I0218497

Israel and The Church

SECOND COMING OF JESUS

ISRAEL AND THE CHURCH

Israel and The Church

SECOND COMING OF JESUS

ISRAEL AND THE CHURCH

LESLIE M. JOHN

Copyright © 1997–2014
Leslie M. John All rights reserved

No part of this book may be reproduced or transmitted in any form or by any means, electronic or mechanical, including photocopying, recording, or by any information storage and retrieval system, without permission in writing from the copyright owner, Leslie M. John.

The entire text in this book, and graphics are protected by Law in US; and internationally according to The Berne Convention 1971

Israel and The Church

My mission is to proclaim the good news of our Lord Jesus Christ as revealed to me through Holy Bible and from various teachers, preachers, and commentators. This is my voluntary service to God in the name of His only begotten Son Lord Jesus Christ.

I share the truth of knowledge of God with others with good intention of bringing them to the knowledge of the living God, the God of Abraham, the God of Isaac, the God of Jacob, and the Father of our Lord Jesus Christ.

My mission is not to convert anyone forcibly to Christianity. One may accept or reject any or part of my writings/teachings. No offense is meant to any individual or any religion or any organization.

All scriptures in electronic format are taken from KJV and Darby Translation by Public Domain, and

New International Version (NIV)

Holy Bible, New International Version®, NIV® Copyright © 1973, 1978, 1984, 2011 by Biblica, Inc. ® Used by permission. All rights reserved worldwide.

English Standard Version (ESV)

The Holy Bible, English Standard Version Copyright © 2001 by Crossway Bibles, a division of Good News Publishers.

Darby Translation (DARBY) by Public Domain

Second Coming of Jesus

Description:

This book deals with the facts about the second coming of Lord Jesus Christ and intriguing questions about "Rapture", "The Restrainer", "Antichrist", "The Two Witnesses", "Armageddon Battle", "New Jerusalem", Israel and the Church, which are two distinct entities, and various Temples described in the Bible.

The sacrifices of Old Testament period are restored to the Israel during millennial kingdom. God promised that David's kingdom will be everlasting. The temple in the millennial kingdom is the promise of God and He will fulfill His covenants viz., Old Covenant, New Covenant, Abrahamic Covenant. Solomon's prayer and answer to his prayer by God, have much significance to understand the plan of God for Israel and the Church.

EBOOK: ISBN-10:098990587X
         ISBN-13: 978-0-9899058-7-9
PRINT MEDIA: ISBN-10: 0989905888
               ISBN-13: 978-0-9899058-8-6

Israel and The Church

Contents

SECOND COMING OF JESUS 3

INTRODUCTION 14

    RAPTURE 16

CHAPTER 1 SEVERITY OF SIN 20

CHAPTER 2 GOD STIRRED UP OUTSIDER 24

CHAPTER 3 GREATNESS UNIMAGINABLE 29

CHAPTER 4 REPATRIATION OF JEWS 33

CHAPTER 5 PROPHETS ADMONISH 38

CHAPTER 6 GOD IS OUR REFUGE 43

CHAPTER 7 THE TEMPLE REBUILT 47

    THE DEDICATION 50

    SOLOMON'S PRAYER 52

    SOLOMON'S PRAYER ANSWERED 52

CHAPTER 8 OBEYING THE LORD 55

Israel and The Church

CHAPTER 9 PAUL AND PERSECUTIONS 59

CHAPTER 10 CONFUSED OVER LETTER 64

CHAPTER 11 THE SEVENTY WEEKS PROPHECY 70

    THE PROPHECY 70

    DANIEL'S CONFESSION 72

    THE DETAILS OF PROPHECY 73

    UNDERSTANDING THE PROPHECY 75

    WHY SEVENTY YEARS? 76

CHAPTER 12 SEVENTY WEEKS – THE TIMING 78

    SIX THINGS DESCRIBED 82

    HOW ONE WEEK EQUALS SEVEN YEARS? 83

    COUNTING DOWN 70 WEEKS PROPHECY 86

    THE DURATION OF SEVENTY YEARS 88

    THE ACTION IN FINAL SEVEN YEARS 88

    SUM UP THE YEARS 89

CHAPTER 13 THE IMPRESSIVE INTERLUDE 90

    REVELATION CHAPTER 7 EXPLALINED 90

THE TEXT	90
EXPOSITION	93
TRIBULATION SAINTS	102
CHAPTER 14 ABOMINATION OF DESOLATION	106
CHAPTER 15 THE ABOMINATION	110
CHAPTER 16 THE DESOLATION	117
CHAPTER 17 ANTICHRIST PART 1	121
CHAPTER 18 JUDAS ISCARIOT BETRAYS	127
CHAPTER 19 ANTICHRIST PART II	131
CHAPTER 20 THE RESTRAINER	136
CHAPTER 21 THE TWO WITNESSES	141
CHAPTER 22 THE LORD IS MIGHTY	151
CHAPTER 23 VESTURE DIPPED IN BLOOD	155
CHAPTER 24 ARMAGEDDON WAR	162
CHAPTER 25 THE FIVE JUDGMENTS	168
THE JUDGMENT AT THE CROSS	168

Israel and The Church

(2) THE JUDGMENT SEAT OF CHRIST.....................171

(3) GREAT TRIBULATION 173

(4) THE JUDGMENT OF NATIONS 175

(5). THE JUDGEMENT OF THE WICKED 179

CHAPTER 26 TEMPLE IN MILLENNIUM 180

CHAPTRER 27 LOOKING TOWARD JERUSALEM......189

CHAPTER 28 GRACE ABOUNDS................................192

   HAS GOD CAST AWAY HIS PEOPLE.......................195

CHAPTER 29 THE FATHER'S LOVE 197

CHAPTER 30 NEW NAME FOR JERUSALEM 203

Second Coming of Jesus

Israel and The Church

INTRODUCTION

The second coming of Lord Jesus is imminent. For a believer, rapture is the second coming of Jesus and for an unbeliever the second appearance of Jesus on the earth is the second coming of Jesus. The prophesies concerning the end times are detailed for us in order that we may have faith and blessed hope of being received by Lord Jesus Christ and be with Him eternally.

The sequence of events leading to the Second coming of Jesus and his establishment of the millennial rule on the earth is disputed among Christians. However the undisputable fact is that the return of the Lord Jesus Christ and the resurrection of the dead saints from their graves followed by the living saints will be caught up is true.

The Pre-tribulation believes that the Church will not face the 'great tribulation' under Antichrist; while the Post-tribulation believes that the Church will face the 'great tribulation' under Antichrist, but will be protected by God.

The doctrine of 'Rapture' of the Church for keeping it away from the 'great tribulation' for seven years is as disputed as the doctrine of rapture of the Church after the 'great tribulation'. The word, 'rapture's is not found in the Scriptures; however in essence the meaning of the said word is getting caught up into the air. The rapture dealing with the believers getting caught up to meet the Lord in the clouds is undisputed among both the groups.

Lord Jesus Christ's purpose of coming again to this earth is two-fold; firstly the second coming is for receiving His own to Himself and secondly, to fulfill the promises made to Israel. Church consisting of saved ones constitutes His bride and the marriage of the bride takes place according to Scriptures after the Church is caught up in the clouds, to meet the Lord in the air. To this marriage between the Lord and His bride are not invited the unsaved ones.

Lord Jesus Christ promised mansions for His Children, who believe in Him. "In my Father's house are many mansions: if it were not so, I would have told you. I go to prepare a place for you (John 14:2). Jesus promised that He was going to heaven to prepare mansions for them. This promise is given in John 14:2 and 3 and this purpose, which was a mystery in the Old Testament, is revealed in the New Testament.

The earthly blessings promised to the children of Israel will be restored unto them when Lord Jesus Christ appears on this earth, while the heavenly blessings promised to His bride are given after the Church is caught up in the clouds to meet the Lord in the air.

After seven years period of Antichrist's rule on the earth during which period unbelievers and Jews undergo God's wrath for having persecuted Jesus when He was on this earth, Jesus makes His second advent on the Mount olives, and later He rules literally for one thousand years sitting on the throne of David fulfilling the prophesies.

The believers constituting His Bride will be always with the Lord. The Church consists of all the believers in Jesus, irrespective of whether they are Jews and Gentiles. The Church consisting of heavenly ones, saved in the precious blood of Lord Jesus Christ is His precious bride. The bride of Christ, which is the Church consisting of blessed ones should not be confused with the Israel. The covenants made to the children of Israel will be fulfilled on this earth. Ref: Acts 1:6, Hebrews 9:28, Romans 11:28, etc. Israel and the Church are separate and if this fact is understood clearly much dispute among Christians about the end days, about 'rapture' will fade away.

RAPTURE

One of the important prophesies that invites our attention, curiosity and hope is about the Second Coming of the Lord

Jesus Christ. Although there is no word, namely, 'rapture' in the Bible, the meaning of this word as presented in 1 Thessalonians 4:17 is 'caught up'.

The Word of God teaches us that Lord Jesus Christ returns physically to establish His Kingdom literally on this earth for one thousand years. Jude 14th verse and 15th verse show us that Enoch prophesied that the Lord will return with ten thousand of His saints to execute judgment upon all. 'Rapture' is the first phase of the Second coming of our Lord Jesus Christ, and in this phase are included all believers in Christ.

'The dead in Christ shall rise first and the living saints shall be caught up together with them in the clouds to meet the Lord in the air'. The blessed hope given to us is that we will be with the Lord for ever.

The resurrection of the dead with the glorified bodies (1 Cor.15:44) will be 'in a moment, in the twinkling of an eye at the last trump: for the trumpet shall sound, and the dead shall be raised incorruptible, and we shall be changed' (1 Cor. 15:52). This happens before the commencement of Daniel's Seventieth week, which is 'great tribulation'.

Israel and The Church

In spite of the differing views about the 'rapture' one view that is consistent with the historical-grammatical interpretation of the Scriptures that survived the test of the time is the view that the living saints at the time of Lord Jesus Christ's second coming will be caught up together with the dead in Christ, who will rise to meet the Lord in the air, every man in the order as presented in 1 Corinthians 15:23 "But every man in his own order: Christ the first-fruits; afterward they that are Christ's at his coming".

"For the Lord himself shall descend from heaven with a shout, with the voice of the archangel, and with the trump of God: and the dead in Christ shall rise first: Then we which are alive and remain shall be caught up together with them in the clouds, to meet the Lord in the air: and so shall we ever be with the Lord". (1 Thessalonians 4:16-17)

There are several reasons to believe that the 'rapture' precedes the 'great tribulation' and that believers in Christ will not see or be part of the 'great tribulation'. Jesus Christ's second coming will be personal and visible. The Lord will descend from heaven with a shout, with the voice of the archangel and with the 'trump of God'.

The Church (Ekklesia) is the precious possession of Lord Jesus Christ and, therefore, it is His love for the Church, and the faithfulness that He has toward His bride that He keeps His bride away from the earthly 'great tribulation', which is primarily for the earthly people and for those, who have rejected Lord Jesus Christ as their Messiah.

Those, who have accepted Jesus as their personal Savior and Lord, by confessing their sins to Him are the treasured possession of Him, and He protects them from the 'great tribulation, which is meant for the children of Israel, who have rejected Jesus as their Messiah. The two-fold purpose of Lord Jesus Christ coming to this earth is to restore the children of Israel their earthly kingdom, which God had promised to their fathers, and also for the heathen to see God's judgment on those, who sinned and rejected Him as their Savior.

The Church always remains with Him with heavenly blessings showered on them by God and are away from the earthly things. That is the reason, why when Lord Jesus Christ descends from heaven in the clouds with a shout, with the voice of archangel, those saints, who are dead in Christ shall rise first and those, who are alive and remain shall be caught up together with them in the clouds, to meet Him in the air, and thereafter we will be with Him for ever.

Israel and The Church

CHAPTER 1 SEVERITY OF SIN

"Whosoever committeth sin transgresseth also the law: for sin is the transgression of the law" (1 John 3:4)

It is hard way to rebuild the ruins. Rebuilding of ruins caused because of disobedience is still hard to build.

God promised children of Israel, as we see in many passages, that He will bless if His children, if they kept His commands and statutes; otherwise He will surely chastise them.

David was blessed because He kept the commands of God but His Solomon drifted away from the commandments of God and His statutes.

Speaking of sin, sinner has no everlasting to be in heaven but will be judged by God to be case into "lake of fire". The sin of believer causes him to be under chastisement from God until he repents of his sin. Nevertheless, the marks of sin in believer's life remain to be visible even after repenting.

Conscience keeps bringing the sins up to memory or before the eyes very often, even though God has already forgiven those sins. The believer keeps struggling to forget the sins he committed or keep Satan away from reminding them to him unless he takes a very strong refuge in the Lord and whisks away Satan in the name of Jesus. God forgives sin, but as long as sinner does not repent he is under the wrath of God and he faces chastisement.

Solomon built a magnificent temple. The walls of the temple inside were overlaid with gold. Because he went astray from God, the temple became a bygone word. First, Sishaq king of Egypt looted the temple of all its glory and wealth. Later Nebuchadnezzar king of Babylon destroyed the city and the temple, which became one of the ancient ruins.

Solomon was king over Israel and his disobedience to the God of Israel not only caused harm to himself but also to the whole nation of Israel. God parted his kingdom into two, which remained at war with each other until Nebuchadnezzar king of Babylon besieged Jerusalem and captured southern kingdom, and later northern kingdom as well. Solomon's temple was leveled to ground and Jews were taken captive by Nebuchadnezzar, who carried them into Babylon .

The Jews remained captive in Babylon for 70 years. Why 70 years? It is because the children of Israel did not keep

Israel and The Church

yearly Sabbath seventy times. The children of Israel worshipped idols, such as Baal and Ashtaroth. The Holy seed mingled with Gentiles and had children by them.

Now, when the children of Israel were in captivity, they cried to the LORD to deliver them from captivity. God told them through prophet Jeremiah that their captivity is for seventy years and they will be redeemed after seventy years are over.

In the meanwhile Jerusalem was in ruins; its walls broken and shattered. Walls show the strength of the city. Walls show the separation; separation of Holy seed from ungodly people.

Even though we are in the world we have a wall of separation from ungodly and wicked. We cannot mingle with them. We are in the world and move along with them socially at work places and in places of business, but we should not have association with sin or sinners and never worship idols, which are abomination to the Lord our God. We worship the living and true God of heaven, the God of Israel, the Father of our Lord Jesus Christ.

"He that committeth sin is of the devil; for the devil sinneth from the beginning. For this purpose the Son of God was manifested, that he might destroy the works of the devil. Whosoever is born of God doth not commit sin; for his seed remaineth in him: and he cannot sin, because he is born of God" (1 John 3:8-9)

Israel and The Church

CHAPTER 2 GOD STIRRED UP OUTSIDER

(Please read my book "Solomon's Temple" This Chapter and following few chapters are about the second Temple.)

"Who is there among you of all his people? his God be with him, and let him go up to Jerusalem, which is in Judah, and build the house of the LORD God of Israel, (he is the God,) which is in Jerusalem" Ezra 1:3

The Book of Nehemiah should be read in conjunction with the Book of Ezra and Book of Esther to get a clear picture of how the decrees were made to build Zerubbabel's Temple, and to restore and to build Jerusalem.

In 1st chapter of the Book of Ezra, Cyrus, king of Persia, inspired by the LORD, issues a decree, so that the word of the LORD by the mouth of Jeremiah should be fulfilled, that the temple at Jerusalem, which was in Judah, should be built (cf. Jeremiah 25:12-14; 29:10; 33:7-13; Daniel 9:1-27; Isaiah 44:28; Esther 1:1-3)

It should be understood clearly that the decree made by Cyrus, the king of Persia was not to build the walls of Jerusalem and restore the city, but to build the temple. The temple was destroyed by Nebuchadnezzar, king of

Babylon; and he took away all the holy vessels from the temple.

The first temple was built by King Solomon and it was a magnificent building with pure gold on the inside of the walls. David, his father had given him much gold, and other vessels to be used in building the temple.

It was because of Solomon's disobedience that God handed over kingdom of Judah, Jerusalem and the temple at Jerusalem into the hands of his adversaries. First, the king of Egypt looted the property from Solomon's Temple, and later Nebuchadnezzar of Babylon destroyed the temple.

The children of Israel from the southern part of Israel, which was called the "House of Judah", were taken captive by King Nebuchadnezzar of Babylon, and they had completed seventy years of captivity in Babylon, when Cyrus made the decree.

God stirred the mind of Cyrus, king of Persia, In order to keep His covenant with David. Cyrus, king of Persia does not belong to the clan of the children of Israel, yet God used Him to fulfill divine plans. Successors of Cyrus

Israel and The Church

namely Cambyses, Darius, and Artexerexes were also not of the genealogy of the children of Israel, yet God used them to fulfill His wishes.

The fathers of Judah and Benjamin, the priests and the Levites, who were inspired by God, went along with first batch of repatriates to Jerusalem to build the temple. They all contributed silver, gold and other goods. It is so wonderful that Cyrus, king of Persia gave them the vessels of the House of the Lord that Nebuchadnezzar carried away when he destroyed the temple. (cf. Ezra 1:5-7)

The rebuilding of the temple began, but soon it stopped for sixteen years, because of the tough opposition, and harassment from adversaries. The adversaries wanted to help those who were building the temple already; but Zerubbabel the son of Shealtiel, governor of Judah, sensed conspiracy and did not allow them to participate in the construction of the Temple. Later, under the decree of Darius rebuilding the temple resumed and the building of the temple was finished on the third day of the month Adar, which was the sixth year of the reign of Darius, the king.

"And this house was finished on the third day of the month Adar, which was in the sixth year of the reign of Darius the king" (Ezra 6:15)

After the temple was built, King Artexerexes, made a decree during his reign that Jerusalem should be rebuilt. The instructions were very specific and comply with the provision in Daniel 9:25, and therefore, the date of his decree is taken as authentic one to count the seventy weeks prophecy.

"Know therefore and understand, that from the going forth of the commandment to restore and to build Jerusalem unto the Messiah the Prince shall be seven weeks, and threescore and two weeks: the street shall be built again, and the wall, even in troublous times" (Daniel 9:25)

When we consider the way God helped His people and the restoration of Jerusalem, it is so amazing that God stirred up those who were outside the clan of Israel to help Israel. Who can be against us if God is with us?

Apostle Paul calls us, the New Testament believers, as more than conquerors through Lord Jesus Christ, who loved us. God, who did not spare His own Son, delivered Him to be bruised on the cross, on behalf of us, is with us. We have salvation through Jesus alone, and the penitent will receive salvation by Grace through faith in Him.

Israel and The Church

Just as God took care of the children of Israel, and stirred up the minds of those, who do not belong to His people, the Lord, will take care of us and fight for us when we are in need. The Lord will help us overcome the powers of devil, and adversaries. He stirs up the minds of those who work against us to work in favor of us.

"...neither death nor life, neither angels nor demons, neither the present nor the future, nor any powers, neither height nor depth, nor anything else in all creation, will be able to separate us from the love of God that is in Christ Jesus our Lord" (cf. Romans 8:38, 39)

CHAPTER 3 GREATNESS UNIMAGINABLE

"When I consider your heavens, the work of your fingers, the moon and the stars, which you have ordained; What is man, that you are mindful of him? and the son of man, that you visit him?" (Psalms 8:3-4)

David praises Jehovah, our master, who has set His glory above the heavens. His name is excellent in all the earth. Several millions of different types of stars, over and above the number of stars that appear to our naked eyes, are magnificently spread across the skies in the constellation. Unless they are viewed through powerful telescopes, they cannot be seen; and it is impossible to view all the stars in the heavens. Our God's abode is far beyond the constellation and his foot-rest is the earth. It is so amazing that such Almighty God lives in our hearts.

Apostle Paul writes:

"There is one glory of the sun, and another glory of the moon, and another glory of the stars: for one star differs from another star in glory" (1 Corinthians 15:41)

Israel and The Church

The LORD has chosen humble, meek, week and those who considered as useless, worthless to proclaim His glory to the proud, haughty, and strong and those who considered them as greatly useful and worthy to possess the assets, knowledge and wisdom.

The preacher in Ecclesiastes considers man's possessions as vanity. The Psalmist says God chose such innocent ones as babes and infants to project the LORD's strength to humble the mighty warriors. Isaiah says no weapon formed against His chosen ones will prevail.

David stands in awe and wonders at the marvelous creation of God, the moon and the stars that the LORD made with his fingers, and ordained them to do their service to mankind. He looks at himself and the mankind, and marvels as to what is man in comparison to such magnificent creation that the Son of man should visit him. He comes to an understanding that God made man little lower than angels and crowned him with glory and honor.

Lord Jesus Christ, the "Son of God", who relinquished His glory, and came to this earth, in the form of a servant in the likeness of man, was called the "Son of man". Psalmist by the inspiration of God considers man, the Lord's creation, as little lower than angels, and so was Lord Jesus Christ, the creator, was made Son of man, a little lower than the angels to suffer death on the cross for the sake of every man's redemption. Salvation is available free of cost to all those who confess Him as the Lord, and believe in heart that God raised Him from death.

"But we see Jesus, who was made a little lower than the angels for the suffering of death, crowned with glory and honor; that he by the grace of God should taste death for every man" (Hebrews 2:9)

The Lord gave power to man to have dominion over the works of the Lord and put all things, even all sheep, oxen, the beasts of the field, fowl of the air, fish of the sea, and whatsoever passes through the paths of the sea, under his feet.

The LORD God made heavens and the earth, and the entire host therein by His word though the breath of His mouth. He gathered waters of the Red Sea together as two heaps one on either side for the children of Israel to walk on dry ground from one end to the other. He lays the depths of the seas in His storehouses, and calms down the storms. He spoke and they came to be. His word is mighty.

Israel and The Church

Psalmist says: "O LORD our Lord, how excellent is your name in all the earth!" Psalm 8:9

The LORD Says:

"For as the heavens are higher than the earth, so are my ways higher than your ways, and my thoughts than your thoughts" (Isaiah 55:9)

CHAPTER 4 REPATRIATION OF JEWS

"Then rose up the chief of the fathers of Judah and Benjamin, and the priests, and the Levites, with all them whose spirit God had raised, to go up to build the house of the LORD which is in Jerusalem" (Ezra 1:5)

The first batch of fifty thousand repatriating Jews was, indeed committed and devoted people to fulfill the desires of the LORD, and they left Babylon after their captivity ended. Cyrus, the King of Persia, issued a decree that whosoever was willing to return to their native land may return and build the temple at Jerusalem, which is in Judah. The Jews willingly accepted the challenges ahead of moved out from their luxuries to hardship in their native land.

Cyrus the king of Persia granted finances to meet the expenses to build the temple. The children of Israel gave to all the workers, the grants of the king, and food. They planned that the cedar trees needed for building the temple could be brought from Lebanon to the sea of Joppa, just as the timber was brought during the days of Solomon when he was building the first temple.

Israel and The Church

The first temple was fully destroyed by Nebuchadnezzar, King of Babylon, more than seventy years before Cyrus issued the decree. The children of Israel quickly arrived in the city of Jerusalem, in the seventh month, and stood in unity as one man to build the temple.

The Jews built the altar and offered burnt offerings morning and evening unto the LORD and according to the Mosaic Law they also kept 'feast of tabernacles' and offered continual burnt offerings, both of the new moons, and all the set feasts, from the first day of the seventh month, and every one offered willingly freewill offerings to the LORD (cf. Leviticus Chapter 23). They had not laid the foundation of the temple yet, because they feared their adversaries and the local people.

Later on, the children of Israel under the leadership of Zerubbabel the son of Shealtiel, the governor of Judah, and Joshua the son of Josedech laid the foundation to build the temple, and the children of Israel rejoiced in the LORD. They sang songs praising the LORD and giving thanks to Him with trumpets, cymbals, after the ordinances of David, the late King of Israel.

Those who had seen in their youth, the grandeur of the first temple built by Solomon, before they were taken captive, were sad and wept aloud with loud voice, when the foundation of the second temple was laid; and many others shouted for joy. Their joy was heard afar off.

The adversaries sent accusations, against the people of Judah and Benjamin, to King The adversaries sent accusations, against the people of Judah and Benjamin, to King Ahesuerus. The accusations were that the city of Jerusalem had a bad record; the inhabitants were rebellious, and did not pay toll, tribute and custom. They charged that they would not pay revenue to the king and made a request that the king may make a search to examine whether or not their charges are true.

> *(Artaxerxes: 1. Was a Persian King Probably identical with AHASUERUS (of Esther 1:1), who prohibited rebuilding of Jerusalem.(Ref. Ezra 4:7-24)*
> *Artaxerxes: 2. Was a King of Persia who decreed in favor of Jews to build Jerusalem (Ezra 7; Nehemiah Chapter 2 and 5:14. (Credits: Nave's Topical Bible))*
>
> *Artexerexes II was Artaxerxes Longimanus, son of Xerxes who reigned from 466-414 B.C. He allowed Nehemiah (Nehemiah 2:1)*

Israel and The Church

> to spend 12 years at Jerusalem to settle the affairs of the returned Jews. He permitted Ezra for 13 years to go on a similar errand. Source: ARTAXERXES [Fausset's Bible Dictionary])

King Artexerxes I made search and found that their allegation about the rebellion of Jews was true, but it was found that they paid toll, tribute and custom to the kings.

However, the king gave a decree that the city of Jerusalem should not be built until, according to him, he would give another command. Thus the work on the temple at Jerusalem came to a halt in the second year of reign of Darius king of Persia. Because of the tough opposition from their adversaries Jews had to stop the work for sixteen years until after Cyrus king of Persia died and Darius was on the throne.

The LORD admonished the children of Israel through prophet Haggai, as detailed in Haggai Chapters 1 and 2, and prophet Zechariah Chapter 1:1-5 that they should build the temple. The LORD promised through the prophets that He will be with them and help them in rebuilding the temple.

The LORD warned the children of Israel in Jerusalem sternly to turn to Him and not behave as their fathers did.

He said to them to turn from their evil ways, and from their evil doings and come to Him. Haggai stressed on them to rebuild the temple.

Zerubbabel the son of Shealtiel, the governor of Judah, and Joshua the son of Josedech, the high priest and the Jews feared the LORD and began building the House of the LORD.

In Acts Chapter 4 we see how Peter and John were imprisoned for speaking boldly and testifying Lord Jesus Christ and even though the priests, captains of the temple, and the Sadducees came against them in opposition they refused to be silent. The believers did unite in prayer and praising the Lord.

When rulers, elders, scribes, Annas the high priest and Caiphas, and John and Alexander questioned peter and John under what authority they were speaking about Jesus and healed a lame man, Peter said:

"Be it known unto you all, and to all the people of Israel, that by the name of Jesus Christ of Nazareth, whom ye crucified, whom God raised from the dead, even by him doth this man stand here before you whole" (Acts 4:10)

Israel and The Church

CHAPTER 5 PROPHETS ADMONISH

"Go up to the mountain, and bring wood, and build the house; and I will take pleasure in it, and I will be glorified, saith the LORD" (Haggai 1:8)

Prophet Haggai admonished the Jews, in the second year of King Darius, on the first day of the sixth month to give careful thought about their negligence in the rebuilding of the temple while they were building their own houses.

First, they set the altar and offered burnt offerings morning and evening unto the LORD. They did not lay the foundations of the temple yet, because of the fear of the local people.

As the work was in progress to build the temple, the adversaries of Judah and Benjamin approached Zerubbabel, and requested that they may also be given chance to participate in the building of the temple. The words they used while seeking permission, to be included in the building process, are noteworthy. They identified the God of Zerubbabel as 'your God'. They said...

"Let us build with you: for we seek your God, as ye do; and we do sacrifice unto him since the days of Esarhaddon king of Assur, which brought us up hither".

Zerubbabel, and Jeshua and the rest of the chiefs of the fathers of Israel quickly sensed conspiracy and said to them…

"Ye have nothing to do with us to build an house unto our God; but we ourselves together will build unto the LORD God of Israel, as king Cyrus the king of Persia hath commanded us"

The conversation among them resulted in confrontation and the people of the land, who were adversaries of Judah and Benjamin, weakened the hands of the people of Judah and caused troubles on purpose, to obstruct the construction of the temple. They went little more ahead and hired counselors and frustrated them with their threats and wrong counsels until Cyrus, king of Persia died, and even until his successor Darius took over reigns as king of Persia.

It was this time when Jews were desperate and were building their homes instead of the House of the LORD. Haggai the prophet and Zechariah the prophet came onto the scene and gave stern warnings to them that they should resume work on the temple.

Israel and The Church

Prophet Haggai said to them that they had excuses in staying inactive from building the temple saying that the time to resume the rebuilding of the temple-work was net yet come. He admonished them saying that they were living in paneled houses, while the House of the LORD was lying waste; the time had come to build the house and it should be built, he said.

Haggai said to them to remember how much God was angry with them when they were disobedient. He reminded them that they had sown much, but reaped very little; although they drank water, yet they did not have enough of it; they wore clothes but there was no warmth in the clothes; they earned wages but their earnings were like saving in a bag with holes.

The prophet warned them that they should consider their ways and go to the mountain and bring wood and build the temple; and he said God promised to take pleasure in their work, and His name will be glorified.

The LORD stirred up the spirit of Zerubbabel, the son of Shealtiel, who was the Governor of Judah, and Joshua the son of Josedech, the high priest and all the people of Judah obeyed the voice of the LORD their God, and Haggai the prophet, and resumed the rebuilding the temple in the twenty fourth day of sixth month of the second year reign of Darius the king. They collected all the material required for rebuilding the temple and laid foundation on the twentieth day of ninth month (Cf. Haggai 2:18)

In the New Testament period there are quite many examples as to how God assured His people to be strong and work for Him. Satan is always at work to disturb the work of the LORD but God assures that He will be with those who work for Him.

Paul was chosen to be minister for Gentiles and he started his ministry amidst great struggles. He went all alone to Philippi where he preached to Lydia, who started church in her own house and when Paul was imprisoned Jailor came to know of Jesus and accepted Him as savior.

In the 1st Century The building of the Church, which is the body of Christ, was not easy but God promised to be with His disciples always. Christ is the head of the Church, and therefore, He rewards those who work for Him.

"Go ye therefore, and teach all nations, baptizing them in the name of the Father, and of the Son, and of the Holy Ghost: Teaching them to observe all things whatsoever I

Israel and The Church

have commanded you: and, lo, I am with you alway, even unto the end of the world. Amen" (Matthew 28:19-20)

Apostle Paul wrote:

"For to me to live is Christ, and to die is gain". (Philippians 1:21)

CHAPTER 6 GOD IS OUR REFUGE

Psalm 46 encourages us that we have God as our rock of refuge and buckler, and a very pleasant help in times of our trouble.

We have no reason to fear that devil would attack us with his wickedness, and would permeate evil through us as long as the LORD is our refuge. The LORD stands like a rock and shield to protect us and He redeems us from all evil and all our enemies.

When the children of Israel faced a giant Assyrian army led by ruthless Sennacherib, who blasphemed the living God, the "angel of the LORD went out and smote in the camp of the Assyrians an hundred fourscore and five thousand" and they were all dead corpses by the morning.

Sennacherib went back to Assyria and lived in Nineveh and when he was worshipping his god his two sons smote him with sword and they escaped into the land of Armenia . And Esarhaddon his son reigned in his stead" (cf. 2 Kings 19:35 -37)

Israel and The Church

Surely, the LORD is our refuge, our strength and a very pleasant help in trouble. Psalmist encourages us in Psalm 2 to worship the Son (which was prophecy about Lord Jesus Christ), and says that all those who put trust in Him are blessed.

Considering the mighty power of the LORD, the psalmist comforts us that even if earth were to be removed from under our feet, and though the mountains are moved out from their places to be cast into the midst of the sea, or the sea roars in storm, yet we have no reason to be afraid of such adverse situations, because God is our rock of refuge.

The favor of the LORD is seen in symbolism used as river water that flows, which make Jerusalem, the holy city of God, and His tabernacles glad.

Psalmist 36:8 refers to rivers of pleasures that the LORD gives us to drink. In Zechariah 14:8 the reference is to the living waters that flow out from Jerusalem, and in Revelation 22:1 John sees in his vision, "a pure river water of life, clear as crystal proceeding out of the throne of God and the Lamb".

The LORD is in the midst of Jerusalem, and the city shall not be moved. God will surely help the city to be restored to its past glory and its name shall be called "Beulah", and even more than that there comes a New Jerusalem out of heaven for believers in Christ to dwell in.

"Thou shalt no more be termed Forsaken; neither shall thy land any more be termed Desolate: but thou shalt be called Hephzibah, and thy land Beulah: for the LORD delighteth in thee, and thy land shall be married" Isaiah 62:4.

Never take pride or lift up horns against the LORD, who can dissolve the earth and the wicked that live therein. Promotion comes neither from east nor west but by Him. God is the judge and He humbles one and He exalts another. He is above all powers in the world and by His word He governs the minds of rulers. (cf. Psalm 75)

The LORD of hosts is with us and the father of our Lord Jesus Christ is always with us. He is our refuge. Look at the desolations He is bringing about by hurricanes and tornadoes, in certain parts of the world, while He is pouring out His anger by drought in another part of the world. He causes wars to cease. He breaks with His bow, the backbone of the pride, and cuts the spears of mighty men into pieces, and He burns the strength of the army of the wicked, and his warfare in the fire of His anger.

Israel and The Church

There is, however, peace and comfort for those who believe in Him, and for those who seek to come under His refuge. The LORD is exalted among all the men and in all the earth. The LORD God of Jacob, who is the Father of our Lord Jesus Christ, is always with us. He is our refuge, strength and a very pleasant help in times of our trouble.

Believe in Lord Jesus Christ. He is the Savior, and there is no name under heaven, where there is salvation.

"Neither is there salvation in any other: for there is none other name under heaven given among men, whereby we must be saved" Acts 4:12

CHAPTER 7 THE TEMPLE REBUILT

Following the request made by the adversaries to continue to stop the work of rebuilding of the second temple at Jerusalem, which was in Judah, Darius the king, made a decree to search for the records. It was customary for the kings during those days to write and preserve their biography, the summary of their reign written in rolls and store them underground in cylinders. Cyrus the king of Persia had one such cylinder with rolls with summary of his reign. A search was ordered by Darius the King and it was to be performed in the house of the rolls, where the treasures were laid up in Babylon.

The search was confined to see if Cyrus the king had made any decree to build the temple; and if so, whether or not the temple work ceased subsequently. The search yielded favorable results and there was found at a place called "Achmetha", which was in the province of Medes, a roll which had the details.

The details in the rolls showed that Cyrus the king of Persia made a decree, in first year of his reign that a house for the God of Israel should be built, a place where they could offer sacrifices to their God and the foundations of the temple be laid strong. The height of the temple, according to his decree, was to be three score cubits, which is about 90 feet, and its breadth equal to that of its height, and with three rows of great stones, and a row of new timber. He ordered that the expenses for construction be met with from the finances of the King's house.

Then Darius the king of Persia ordered that the vessels, which king Nebuchadnezzar carried away from the first temple, when the latter conquered Jerusalem, be brought to Babylon and thereafter every vessel to be restored to its place in the temple at Jerusalem, which was in Judah.

Darius the king ordered the adversaries of Jews to stay away from hindering the temple-construction. He decreed to commence rebuilding of the temple under the supervision of the Jews and the elders of the Jews. In his decree the king ordered the entire expenses that may incur for the construction of the temple be given from the king's possession, without fail and without causing any obstruction; and also to provide young bullocks, rams, and lambs, and also wheat, salt, wine and oil to meet their needs of offering of burnt offerings to their God of heavens as desired by the priests. The king's ardent desire was that they may offer sacrifices of sweet savors unto the God of heaven, and pray for his good health and for his sons.

King Darius decreed that the rebuilding of the temple be done with speed and ordered severe punishment for anyone, who may alter his word or cause obstruction to the construction of the temple. He decreed that whoever alters his word may be hung unto death from the timber that may be pulled down from the house of the one that causes obstruction, and thereafter, the house may be made a dunghill. He also wrote that the God who caused His name to dwell there would destroy all kings and people, who put their hand to alter and to destroy the house of God at Jerusalem.

Tatnai the governor and Shetharboznai and their companions did carry out the work speedily in compliance to the decree made by Darius the king. The elders of the Jews built the temple according to the commandment of the God of Israel, and according to the commandments of Cyrus, Darius, and Artaxerxes kings of Persia. They rebuilt the temple and prospered as prophesied by prophets Haggai and Zechariah.

The rebuilding of the house of God was finished on the third day of the month Adar, in the sixth year of reign of king Darius.

Israel and The Church

THE DEDICATION

On the third day of the Jewish month Adar in the sixth year of the reign of Darius the king of Persia the temple building was completed. It was a joyous occasion for the children of Israel, the priests, and the Levites as also of the rest of the children of Israel who were still in captivity in Babylon.

When the temple building was completed there was in Jerusalem only the first batch of fifty thousand repatriates of the children of Israel. The next two batches repatriated later; the second batch along with Ezra, who was a scribe of the Law of Moses and a priest, and the third batch along with Nehemiah the cup-bearer of King Artexerxes. The temple dedication was grand when they offered an hundred bullocks, two hundred rams, four hundred lambs. They also offered as sin offering twelve he goats, according to the number of the tribes of Israel.

The children of Israel, now before the second temple, set the priests in their divisions and the Levites in their courses for the service of God in the temple. Everything was done according the Law written in the book of Moses. They kept the Passover on the fourteenth day of the first month Nisan. The priests and the Levites purified themselves. They had concern for their brethren, the priests and themselves, and therefore, they killed Passover for not only those who were present at the time of dedication of the second temple, but also on behalf of the children of Israel, who were still under captivity.

The rest of the children of Israel came to Jerusalem from their captivity in Babylon in due course of time and they separated themselves from the filthiness of the heathen of the land, and sought the LORD God of Israel and kept Passover and ate of it. They also kept the feast of the 'unleavened bread' for seven days as it is written in the book of Moses. They rejoiced in the LORD and joyful because He turned the King of Assyria unto their favor and for strengthening their hands in the work of the House of God, the God of Israel.

Nevertheless, all the Jews never returned to Jerusalem. Many Jews settled in Persia because they felt comfortable there. The "House of Israel" was scattered and it is in the knowledge of the Almighty God where the children of Israel who belonged to the 'House of Israel" are now. The entire House of Judah is yet to go back to their native land.

Israel and The Church

SOLOMON'S PRAYER

It is worth recalling the dedication of the *first temple built by Solomon* the great King of Israel. His prayer was very humble and appealing. He submitted his supplications to the LORD, and in his prayer he urged the LORD to forgive the sins of the children of Israel, if they cry unto the LORD repenting of their sins, in their troubles in future, turning their faces towards Jerusalem. The children of Israel were taken captive and cried to the LORD for mercy. It is also noteworthy that Daniel prayed confessing the sins of the children of Israel three times a day looking towards Jerusalem from the window of his chamber. The LORD forgave them and brought them to the land of Jerusalem after their captivity for seventy years were fulfilled. (cf. 1 Kings 8:22-53)

Now when Daniel knew that the writing was signed, he went into his house; and his windows being open in his chamber toward Jerusalem, he kneeled upon his knees three times a day, and prayed, and gave thanks before his God, as he did aforetime. (Daniel 6:10)

SOLOMON'S PRAYER ANSWERED

The LORD confirmed His answer to Solomon's prayer of dedication of the first temple i.e. Solomon's temple, at

Jerusalem by sending fire that came down from heaven and consumed the burnt offering and sacrifices. Fire coming down and consuming the offering indicated God's acceptance of the offering.

Solomon's sacrifice was exorbitant. He offered twenty thousand oxen and hundred thousand and twenty thousand sheep at the time of dedicating the house of the LORD. Here is an important point to note.

The sacrifices that Solomon offered were more in number than the brazen altar could accommodate and, therefore, he sanctified and consecrated the middle of the court that was before the LORD. This kind of huge sacrifice was never offered before when the children of Israel were on their journey in the wilderness for forty years.

Solomon prayed to the LORD hallowing the middle court for offering sacrifices God answered his prayer and accepted the said place i.e. the middle of the court as a place of offering in addition to brazen altar.

The priests waited on their offerings and sounded the trumpets and the Levites played music and all the children of Israel stood before the LORD as a mark of honoring the

Israel and The Church

LORD. Solomon celebrated the feast for seven days and all the children of Israel participated in the festival and were joyous.

The LORD appeared to Solomon by night and confirmed that He heard Solomon's prayer and chose the place for Himself as a house of sacrifice. The LORD also detailed His answer to each petition submitted by Solomon. The LORD said:

"If my people, which are called by my name, shall humble themselves, and pray, and seek my face, and turn from their wicked ways; then will I hear from heaven, and will forgive their sin, and will heal their land" (2 Chronicles 7:14)

The LORD did not leave them too comfortable but put a condition that they should keep His statutes and commandments; otherwise, He will "pluck them up by the roots out of my land which I have given them; and this house, which I have sanctified for my name, will I cast out of my sight, and will make it to be a proverb and a byword among all nations" (cf. 2 Chronicles 7:19-20)

CHAPTER 8 OBEYING THE LORD

"Be glad in the LORD, and rejoice, ye righteous: and shout for joy, all ye that are upright in heart"   Psalm 32:11

David comforts his own soul, as he does of others, when he says that those, whose sins are forgiven, are blessed. Truly, he has a definite reason to say that he was blessed inasmuch he was forgiven by God of the transgression of the law. He did that which was evil in the sight of the LORD. It was of adultery with Bathsheba and conspiracy against her husband, Uriah and much later of numbering his army. Except for the grace of God he had no chance of being blessed in his life.

The thing that pleased God, of David was that the he repented of his sin, besides obeying the LORD's commands with regard to wiping away the enemies of Israel from the face of the earth.

"After removing Saul, he made David their king. God testified concerning him: 'I have found David son of Jesse, a man after my own heart; he will do everything I want him to do.'" Acts 13"22

Israel and The Church

On the contrary, King Saul's performance as king over Israel was much unpleasant to the LORD, because he showed his own wisdom and priorities to prevail as against God's desires. Saul did not wipe away Amalekites fully from the face of the earth in spite of the fact that he had unflinching support from God.

"And the LORD sent thee on a journey, and said, Go and utterly destroy the sinners the Amalekites, and fight against them until they be consumed" (1 Samuel 15:18)

"For rebellion is as the sin of witchcraft, and stubbornness is as iniquity and idolatry. Because thou hast rejected the word of the LORD, he hath also rejected thee from being king" (1 Samuel 15:23)

David's procrastination in confessing his sin exceedingly troubled him in his heart, and he groaned many a day, the entire day. Day and night God's hand weighed very heavy on him, and his strength waxed weak. His health continually deteriorated as if water in his body evaporated due to the heat of the summer.

David knew that if he confessed his sins, the LORD does not hold them against him and he knew that God will not hold him responsible of his sins because he repented of his sin, and had no deceit in his heart. David's comfort arose from the decision he made that read "I will confess my transgressions to the Lord".

No sooner than David acknowledged his sin before the LORD, refraining further from continuing to hide it from the LORD, he was sure that his guilt of sinning against the LOD was forgiven.

David, after receiving assurance of his salvation, desires that all the faithful may pray to the LORD, while he may be found. He seeks from others the same attitude of confessing their sins to the LORD.

The LORD is night unto them that seek Him and He is their shelter to hide them under His wings. He protects us from trouble and causes us to praise Him with songs of deliverance.

Therefore, David says a man should not be rebellious. The LORD will teach us the way we should tread on. The LORD gives us His counsel with His loving eye on us. He advises us not be like horse or as the mule that have no understanding but must be controlled with bit and bridle lest they hurt us.

Israel and The Church

Many are the afflictions of wicked, but the LORD is near to them that seek Him. There is reason for the righteous and upright in heart to rejoice in the Lord and be glad in Him and sing unto Him praises continually.

"Be ye not as the horse, or as the mule, which have no understanding: whose mouth must be held in with bit and bridle, lest they come near unto thee". Psalm 32:9

Jesus said:

"Come unto me, all ye that labour and are heavy laden, and I will give you rest". (Matthew 11:28)

CHAPTER 9 PAUL AND PERSECUTIONS

"And I punished them oft in every synagogue, and compelled them to blaspheme; and being exceedingly mad against them, I persecuted them even unto strange cities" (Acts 26:11)

Apostle Paul testifies before King Agrippa as to how he went before his conversion to Damascus with authority and commission from chief priests to persecute Christians and the Church and says to him "At midday, O king, I saw in the way a light from heaven, above the brightness of the sun, shining round about me and them which journeyed with me. And when we were all fallen to the earth, I heard a voice speaking unto me, and saying in the Hebrew tongue, Saul, Saul, why persecutest thou me? it is hard for thee to kick against the pricks. And I said, Who art thou, Lord? And he said, I am Jesus whom thou persecutes"

Lord Jesus Christ called Apostle Paul to be a minister and witness both of those things that he has seen and to deliver him from people, and from Gentiles, unto whom he was sent with the Gospel of Jesus Christ (cf. Acts 26:11-19)

Later in his life Apostle Paul faced persecutions and God was with him. He was beaten up and persecuted at Philippi when he preached Gospel of Jesus Christ and was imprisoned. Later, the authorities let him go, but Paul demanded that sergeants must themselves come and release him because he was a Roman citizen and did no wrong.

The magistrates and sergeants feared and requested Paul to leave Philippi. Thus Paul left Philippi and went to Thessalonica via Amphipolis and Apollonia. Paul established church at Thessalonica. Silas (also called Silvanus) and Timothy (also called Timotheus) helped him in his ministry. Paul reasoned three Sabbath days in the Synagogues at Thessalonica debating with them on intriguing questions about Jesus Christ, his death, burial, resurrection, and His second coming (Ref. Acts 17:1-5)

Contrary to the beliefs of Jews at Thessalonica, Paul said he preached Christ, who was crucified, died and rose from the dead. Some of them, who believed his preaching, was a great multitude from devout Greeks and women, but Jews, who did not believe his preaching were moved with envy and with the help of some "lewd fellows of baser sort" and gathered a company and not only caused uproar in the city but also assaulted the house of one named Jason.

Interest grew in people of the land and gathered more and more to listen to Paul's preaching. Seeing that Paul is gathering much importance Jews in Thessalonica were jealous and tried to harm him.

The brethren at Thessalonica sensed the trouble caused by the obstructionists and sent Paul, Silas, and Timothy by night to Berea where Paul preached Gospel to brethren at Berea in the synagogues of Jews (Ref. Acts 17:10, 18)

The believers at Berea were more interested to learn the word of God than Thessalonians. They received the word of God with all readiness but did not just believe anything preached or taught to them without searching the scriptures daily if the preaching or teaching was according to the word of God.

There is lesson for us here that we should not take every teaching as granted without referring to the scriptures if it were really so. Many times it so happens that listeners or readers are misguided by false teachings by emotional preaching and teaching. Bible warns us not to be taken away by false preachers or false teachings.

Many people at Berea believed Jesus Christ, as the Son of God, as preached by Paul and among those who believed were honorable women who were Greeks, and many men.

Paul faced similar circumstances as he faced at Thessalonica when Jews from Thessalonica went to Berea and stirred up people against him. Then the brethren at Berea sent away Paul to go as it were to the sea but led him from there to Athens. Paul preferred to be alone at Athens considering the ministry that was to be carried on by Silas and Timothy at Berea.

"And then immediately the brethren sent away Paul to go as it were to the sea: but Silas and Timotheus abode there still" (Acts 17:14)

After-a-while Paul sent word for Silas and Timothy to join him in his ministry and Paul went to Corinth. When Silas and Timothy joined Paul at Corinth, he sent Timothy back to Thessalonica to comfort the believers at Thessalonica and also to bring a report as to how they were doing in the Lord.

It is evident from Paul's ministry in the first century that persecutions did not hinder the growth of the Church; but rather the Churches increased and the Gospel of Jesus Christ was preached in many parts of the world. It was then true and it is now true that whenever the church is persecuted it thrived and grew rather than diminishing. God never allows the Church to diminish or to be destroyed. It is those who persecute the Church who will, eventually, be destroyed.

Israel and The Church

CHAPTER 10 CONFUSED OVER LETTER

"And to wait for his Son from heaven, whom he raised from the dead, even Jesus, which delivered us from the wrath to come" (1 Thessalonians 1:10)

Apostle Paul wrote two letters to Thessalonians from Corinth. First letter included doctrines, related to the Gospel of Lord Jesus Christ, in word, in power and in the Holy Spirit. The important aspect of the Gospel of Jesus Christ that Paul emphasized in his first letter was that Lord Jesus was raised from the dead, and delivered us from the wrath that was to come upon us. Secondly, he asked Thessalonians, as also us, to wait for Jesus, who will surely come again. This doctrine was very hard for Thessalonians to understand and, therefore, they were filled with confusion and were worried.

In the meanwhile the Thessalonians received a fake letter, from some unknown source, causing much disturbance in their belief about Lord Jesus Christ's second coming. In the letter purportedly written by Paul, it was, perhaps, stated that the day of Christ was already at hand, obviously causing confusion in their minds about the destiny of their forefathers who died before them, and their own status on the earth as of that date.

"That ye be not soon shaken in mind, or be troubled, neither by spirit, nor by word, nor by letter as from us, as that the day of Christ is at hand. Let no man deceive you by any means: for that day shall not come, except there come a falling away first, and that man of sin be revealed, the son of perdition" (2 Thessalonians 2:2-3)

It was, therefore, necessary for Paul to write a second letter to Thessalonians that every letter, dictated by him, and written by someone else on behalf of him, was personally signed by him, endorsing that the letter was from him and it had the contents revealed to him by Lord Jesus Christ.

Paul included the names of Silvanus (also known as Silas), and Timotheus (also known as Timothy) and wished them Grace and peace from God our Father and Lord Jesus Christ.

It is worth noting that Paul places the Father and the Son on the same level much to thwart the confusion of those who consider the Son as not equal to the Father. He

Israel and The Church

infuses much confidence in Thessalonians that they were called by God and wishes them grace and peace.

"Grace unto you, and peace, from God our Father and the Lord Jesus Christ" (2 Thessalonians 1:2)

Paul clarifies in his letters to Thessalonians that Lord Jesus Christ will come only after the 'man of sin', the 'son of perdition' is revealed first. He says that the Lord will come to be 'glorified in his saints and be admired in all them that believe'.

Paul was happy that his testimony about Lord Jesus Christ was believed by the hearers. He says that they will see Lord Jesus face to face when the Lord comes again. Paul comforts them that he and his companions will pray always for them that they may be counted worthy of the calling of our Lord Jesus, and to fulfill His good pleasure, and the work of faith with power. He praises our Lord Jesus Christ and wishes that the Lord's name may be glorified in them, and also that their faith in the Lord may stand firm, according to the grace of our God and the Lord Jesus Christ.

Timothy, who visited Thessalonica from Corinth, at the behest of Paul, to comfort them and also bring news about them to Paul, gave report to the latter that Thessalonians were increasing in the knowledge of God exceedingly, and their love toward one another abounded. However, the report did not contain their status about their 'patience of hope' in Lord Jesus Christ's second coming (cf. 1 Thessalonians 1:3; 2 Thessalonians 1:2; 1 Thessalonians 3:6). This was obviously because Paul received information, perhaps by an anonymous letter, about their confusion in the doctrine that he preached.

Thessalonians thought that Paul was praising them not from his heart. This doubt in the minds of Thessalonians prompted Paul to reiterate, in his second letter, that Paul was, indeed thankful to God about their spiritual growth and about their abounding love toward one another. Paul said he, Silas and Timothy were bound to give thanks to God for them, and it was fitting to praise them because their faith grew exceedingly and their love towards one another abounded in spite of their endurance of persecutions and tribulations (Ref. 2 Thessalonians 1:3)

Paul's desire was that they should count themselves worthy of the kingdom of God even as they suffer tribulations and persecutions, which are nothing but the result of the righteous judgment of God. They are assured

Israel and The Church

that God's wrath pours on those, who do not accept the Gospel of Jesus Christ.

Those who reject Jesus as their savior will suffer 'great tribulation' when Lord Jesus Christ will be revealed from heaven with His mighty angels. Those who reject Jesus Christ and His Gospel will be punished with everlasting destruction, when He comes again to rule the kingdoms with the rod of iron.

Once the Lord Jesus Christ came as a Lamb of God and died on behalf of sinners that they may receive salvation free of cost by accepting Him as savior. All those who confess their sins to Lord Jesus Christ and accept Him as personal Savior will receive everlasting life to be with Him for ever and ever, and all those who reject Him as Savior will be punished with everlasting destruction from the presence of the Lord, and from the glory of His power. (cf. Romans 3:23; Romans 6:23 and Romans 10:9; and 2 Corinthians 5:21)

"For he hath made him to be sin for us, who knew no sin; that we might be made the righteousness of God in him". (2 Corinthians 5:21)

The very first message from Apostle Peter to the Church contained David's hope in the Lord, even before the Lord was born that his heart rejoiced, and his tongue was glad that his flesh will rest in hope because the LORD will neither leave his soul in hell nor will He suffer Lord Jesus the Holy One to see corruption.

We, as believers in the Lord Jesus Christ have the assurance that we will rise from the dead and our future will be with the Lord Jesus Christ for ever and ever. (Ref. 1Thessalonians 4:16-17)

"Therefore did my heart rejoice, and my tongue was glad; moreover also my flesh shall rest in hope: Because thou wilt not leave my soul in hell, neither wilt thou suffer thine Holy One to see corruption". (Acts 2:26-27)

CHAPTER 11 THE SEVENTY WEEKS PROPHECY

THE PROPHECY

Seventy weeks are determined upon thy people and upon thy holy city, to finish the transgression, and to make an end of sins, and to make reconciliation for iniquity, and to bring in everlasting righteousness, and to seal up the vision and prophecy, and to anoint the most Holy. Daniel 9:24

Know therefore and understand, that from the going forth of the commandment to restore and to build Jerusalem unto the Messiah the Prince shall be seven weeks, and threescore and two weeks: the street shall be built again, and the wall, even in troublous times. Daniel 9:25

And after threescore and two weeks shall Messiah be cut off, but not for himself: and the people of the prince that shall come shall destroy the city and the sanctuary; and the end thereof shall be with a flood, and unto the end of the war desolations are determined. Daniel 9:26

And he shall confirm the covenant with many for one week: and in the midst of the week he shall cause the sacrifice and the oblation to cease, and for the overspreading of abominations he shall make it desolate, even until the consummation, and that determined shall be poured upon the desolate. Daniel 9:27

Daniel writes that while he was speaking and praying to the LORD, confessing his sin and the sin of the people of Israel, Gabriel the mighty angel of the LORD appeared to him in vision, and said to him that he came to Daniel to give an insight and understanding. The angel said that as soon as he began to pray, a word, obviously from the LORD, went out that he should go and tell Daniel that he was highly esteemed, and therefore, he came to reveal the prophecy about the restoration of Israel.

Israel suffered tremendous displeasure from the LORD during the days of King Solomon, who married wives from heathen nations, against the will of the LORD, and had concubines. Solomon, who was loved by God greatly, was put to severe chastisement and his kingdom was divided. However, there was a covenant that the LORD could not break. The covenant was that David's kingdom will last for ever and ever and if Solomon committed sin, he would be chastised by God's mercy shall not depart from him.

Israel and The Church

Consequent upon Solomon's transgression his kingdom was divided into two. The Northern kingdom was called the "House of Israel" with ten tribes, and the southern kingdom was called the "House of Judah" with two tribes namely Judah and Benjamin. Levites, who were priests assimilated into both the houses.

The children of Israel also resorted to idolatry thus dishonoring God. Their disobedience resulted in God getting angry, and sending them into captivity under king Nebuchadnezzar of Babylon for seventy years. Babylonians under the leadership of king Nebuchadnezzar attacked southern kingdom of Israel and looted Solomon's Temple, which was so elegant in construction that it had gold all over the inner walls of the temple. They also destroyed whole of Jerusalem.

Later, Babylonians conquered Assyrians in the northern part of Israel also and took full control of Israel. They carried the children of Israel captive.

DANIEL'S CONFESSION

Daniel, in captivity, prayed to the LORD on behalf of the children of Israel three times every day with the window towards Jerusalem open.

During the days of Solomon, on the day of dedication of Solomon's temple, Solomon prayed to the LORD to forgive the children of Israel if children of Israel faced towards Jerusalem and confessed their sins in prayer to the LORD. The LORD promised to Solomon that if the children of Israel confessed their sins to the LORD with their faces toward Jerusalem, He will forgive them of their transgressions and sins.

While they were in captivity, Daniel sought from the LORD an answer as to how long they would be in captivity. God answered by the mouth of His mighty angel, Gabriel that seventy years were determined upon them and they would release in full will be after the completion of seventy years.

THE DETAILS OF PROPHECY

Seventy sevens were determined for the people of Israel, and for the holy city, Jerusalem, to finish transgression and to put an end to sin that they committed. This duration of this period was determined by the LORD to atone for their wickedness and to bring in everlasting righteousness. Daniel was asked to seal up the prophecy and to anoint the Most Holy Place.

Israel and The Church

Daniel's Seventy Weeks prophecy as it is commonly known, is a very important and interesting prophecy, which the LORD declared by the mouth of angel Gabriel to Daniel, the prophet. This prophecy basically unveils God's dealing with Israel, the future of Israel and their restoration.

Inasmuch as the Church came into existence when Israel rejected Lord Jesus as their Messiah, this prophecy also unveils the future of Church. However, Israel and the Church are exclusive and do not participate in one another's dealings and blessings. There is remarkable advantage of being in the Church. There is no difference between Jew or Gentile and everyone will have glorified bodies, and will be conformed to the image of Jesus Christ and will live for ever and ever.

With the Church coming into existence the continuity of seventy-week prophecy is broken at 69th week. At the end of 69th week Lord Jesus Christ descends "from heaven with a shout, with the voice of the archangel, and with the trump of God: and the dead in Christ shall rise first: Then we which are alive and remain shall be caught up together with them in the clouds, to meet the Lord in the air: and so shall we ever be with the Lord". (1 Thessalonians 4:16-17)

Thereafter Daniel's prophecy of seventieth-week commences and in the midst of seven-year period, Antichrist breaks his covenant with Israel and for the remaining portion of three and half years Israel will suffer under great tribulation (Ref. Revelation Chapter 7)

UNDERSTANDING THE PROPHECY

Angel Gabriel told Daniel to know and understand that from the time the word goes out to restore and rebuild the Jerusalem until the Anointed One, the ruler comes there will be seven sevens and sixty-two sevens. While the Jerusalem and the temple being rebuilt, the Anointed One, the Ruler will be put to death after sixty-two sevens. The people will destroy the city and the sanctuary. The end comes like a flood and war continues until the end and desolations will be decreed. The Antichrist will confirm a covenant of peace for seven years and in the middle of seven-year-period, i.e at the beginning of the later 3 ½ years Antichrist will declare himself as God and sits in the most holy place of the temple, he will put an end to sacrifices and oblations. He will set up, in the temple, an abomination which causes desolation until the end that is decreed is poured on him.

Israel and The Church

WHY SEVENTY YEARS?

The children of Israel violated seventy times God's command of giving the land rest for one year after every six years. This intermission in farming and giving rest to the land was according to the LORD and it was meant to help poor to glean for one year from the land left-over of the harvest at the end of sixth year. It was also meant to honor God's word.

And six years thou shalt sow thy land, and shalt gather in the fruits thereof: But the seventh year thou shalt let it rest and lie still; that the poor of thy people may eat: and what they leave the beasts of the field shall eat. In like manner thou shalt deal with thy vineyard, and with thy oliveyard. (Exodus 23:10-11)

God gave command to the children of Israel that they may sow the land for six years and gather fruits thereof, but they should let the land rest and lie still on the seventh year. Not only God had concern for the rich among the children of Israel but He had concern for the poor among the children of Israel, as well. He said to them to that they should allow the poor among them to eat and gather from the land the seventh year. Likewise they were also asked to allow beasts of the field to eat. Similarly, they were commanded to leave their vineyards and olive yards lie rest the seventh year for the poor and the beast to eat thereof. However, the children of Israel violated God's command.

CHAPTER 12 SEVENTY WEEKS – THE TIMING

King Cyrus of Persia had the knowledge of Jeremiah's prophecy concerning the destruction of Babylon and this is evident from his own confession as it is written in Ezra 1:1-4

Whether it is the heart of a king or a subject in his kingdom the LORD has the control over his heart and the LORD's plans prevail always. It was time for Jews to return to Jerusalem, and the LORD rose up Cyrus, the king of Persia to achieve His plans.

The LORD stirred up the spirit of Cyrus, king of Persia, who made proclamation, in his first year of reign that the LORD God of has given all the kingdoms of the earth, and charged him that he should to build a house for the LORD at Jerusalem, in the kingdom of Judah. This proclamation was in fulfillment of Jeremiah's prophecy in Jeremiah 25:12-14.

According to Jeremiah prophecy the LORD will punish king of Babylon after seventy years captivity of Israel is accomplished and the LORD God will recompense great kings according to their deeds and their works. Cyrus had these thoughts in his mind when he made proclamation.

He ordered that Jews may return to their native land and rebuild the temple. Solomon's temple was destroyed by Nebuchadnezzar, king of Babylon when he sieged the Holy City and robbed all the vessels, gold and other sanctified items.

The destruction of Jerusalem and of Solomon's temple was in the plan of God, who ordered so, when Solomon defied the LORD's statutes. The LORD had said to him that he should walk in His statutes and if he disobeyed the LORD and broke the statutes, the grandeur of the temple will be a by-gone word in the mouth of people who behold it.

And Nebuchadnezzar king of Babylon came against the city, and his servants did besiege it. And Jehoiachin the king of Judah went out to the king of Babylon, he, and his mother, and his servants, and his princes, and his officers: and the king of Babylon took him in the eighth year of his reign. And he carried out thence all the treasures of the house of the LORD, and the treasures of the king's house, and cut in pieces all the vessels of gold which Solomon king of Israel had made in the temple of the LORD, as the LORD had said. (2 Kings 24:11-13)

Israel and The Church

The children of Judah, and Benjamin and Levites who were with them cried unto the LORD for mercy. Daniel prayed to the LORD three times every day with the window in his room opened towards Jerusalem.

Nebuchadnezzar captured Jerusalem and took away the 'House of Judah' captive to Babylon and it should have ended with the return of Jews, but they did not return in full. The restoration of Israel is yet future. Obviously the Church has come in the midst of the seventy week prophecy. The church began in Acts Chapter 2 and the grace period, as it is commonly called, is not yet over. It thwarts away all theories, opinions, and assumptions of assigning the definite starting point of time and ending point of time of the seventy weeks. If the seventy weeks have already been completed, then the prophecy in the Book of Revelation seems to be redundant. The book of Revelation is still in the Bible and it says these are future events.

It is hard to substantiate the view that seventy week prophecy is completed. The entire future and the prophecies about various temples, and the return of Lord Jesus Christ, do not permit us to believe that the seventieth week is complete.

Second Coming of Jesus

"Heaven and earth shall pass away, but my words shall not pass away. But of that day and hour knoweth no man, no, not the angels of heaven, but my Father only" (Matthew 24:35-36)

The overview of the structure of the book of Revelation reveals the following phases.

1. Chapter 1 – The glorified Christ – Resurrected Christ in His glory
2. Chapter 2 and 3 – The Churches - messages from Christ to seven literal churches and represents the Church in general
3. Chapters 4 & 5 Heavenly throne room. The Church after rapture serves and worship the Lord.
4. Chapters 6-19 seventieth week of Daniel - Further breakup is …

   Chapters 6-9 The first three and half years have the details of the seals, judgments and the trumpet judgments
   Chapters 10, 11, 12, 13 and14 have the details of the middle of tribulation period
   Chapter 11 shows Reconstruction of temple, and

ministry of two witnesses

Chapter 12 has the details of Water in heaven

Chapter 13 has the details of Rise of Antichrist

5. Chapters 15-18 have the details of Last three and half years - Bowl judgments, destruction of Commercial Babylon, and Religious Babylon
6. Chapter 19 have the details of the Return of Lord Jesus Christ

    Chapter 20 have the details of Millennium and the last judgment
7. Chapters 21 and 22 have the details of New heaven and New earth

The Book of Revelation is clear that the seventieth week of Prophecy is yet future. Daniel's seventy-week prophecy is seen in Daniel Chapter 9:24-27

Daniel 9:24 lists six things to be achieved in seventy weeks.

SIX THINGS DESCRIBED

Seventy weeks are determined upon thy people and upon thy holy city, to finish the transgression, and to make an end of sins, and to make reconciliation for iniquity, and to bring in everlasting righteousness, and to seal up the vision and prophecy, and to anoint the most Holy. (Daniel 9:24)

1. to finish the transgression, and
2. to make an end of sins, and
3. to make reconciliation for iniquity, and
4. to bring in everlasting righteousness, and
5. to seal up the vision and prophecy, and
6. to anoint the most Holy.

HOW ONE WEEK EQUALS SEVEN YEARS?

According to Bible the number of days in a week while reckoning them for a specific purpose is a day is equal to a year. The children of Israel murmured against the LORD and angered Him and, therefore, God said that they would wander 40 years in the wilderness equal to 40 days of their search of the land.

And they returned from searching of the land after forty days. (Numbers 13:25)

Israel and The Church

And your children shall wander in the wilderness forty years, and bear your whoredoms, until your carcases be wasted in the wilderness. After the number of the days in which ye searched the land, even forty days, each day for a year, shall ye bear your iniquities, even forty years, and ye shall know my breach of promise. (Numbers 14:33-34)

Interestingly at several places in the Bible 40 is considered as a testing number/period.

In a surprising design God provided bearing of iniquity of children of Israel by saying to Ezekiel, the prophet, to take a tile and lay it before him and portray upon it a city, the holy city of Jerusalem and make an attempt to capture it, "and build forts against it, and cast a mound against it, and set camps against it, and place battering-rams against it roundabout"

Then, God said to Ezekiel to take an iron plate, and set it as a wall between him and the city and, thereafter set his face against it, and it shall be besieged, and he shall make attempt to capture it. It shall be a sign to the "House of Israel".

And God said Ezekiel should bear the iniquity of the "House of Israel" for three hundred and ninety days as the LORD "appointed him years of iniquity, according the number of days"

I have appointed thee the years of their iniquity, according to the number of the days. In addition, in Ezekiel 4:6 we see that he should bear the iniquity of the house of Judah for forty days, which God appointed as one day for a year.

Another reference is about the numbering seven Sabbaths of years is seven times seven years and the gap between seven Sabbaths of years shall be forty nine years.

"And thou shalt number seven sabbaths of years unto thee, seven times seven years; and the space of the seven sabbaths of years shall be unto thee forty and nine years". (Leviticus 25:8)

Another logical reasoning is that Nehemiah 6:15 says building of walls was completed in 52 days. If a week is considered as seven days and not seven years, then seven weeks equal to 49 days, which is totally impossible number of days to build the temple.

God's calendar had 30 days in a month. Three and half years equal to 1260 days or 42 months. Seven years equal to 2520 days not 2521.75 days@ 365.25 days in a year.

Israel and The Church

COUNTING DOWN 70 WEEKS PROPHECY

The counting of the seventy weeks prophecy is recorded in Daniel 9:25. It commences when the decree was issued to restore and to build Jerusalem. Duration from the date the decree went out until its completion, with all interferences and objections in the meanwhile, was 49 years. That is seven weeks of years i.e. 7x7=49 years.

Know therefore and understand, that from the going forth of the commandment to restore and to build Jerusalem unto the Messiah the Prince shall be seven weeks, and threescore and two weeks: the street shall be built again, and the wall, even in troublous times. (Daniel 9:25)

Now in the first year of Cyrus king of Persia, that the word of the LORD by the mouth of Jeremiah might be fulfilled, the LORD stirred up the spirit of Cyrus king of Persia, that he made a proclamation throughout all his kingdom, and put it also in writing, saying, Thus saith Cyrus king of Persia, The LORD God of heaven hath given me all the kingdoms of the earth; and he hath charged me to build him an house at Jerusalem, which is in Judah. (Ezra 1:1-2)

Another opinion is when Artaxerxes, King of Persia issued a decree. Most acceptable view is the decree by Artexerexes. (Cf. Nehemiah 2:1-8). The phrase "commandment to restore and to build Jerusalem" in the prophecy is very important to evaluate the decrees. The decree from Cyrus contained return of Jews to their land and to build the Temple; it did not contain the vital phrase of the prophecy, which is "to restore and to build Jerusalem". The decree from Darius was no more than a repetition of the decree from Cyrus. The decree of Artexerexes matched perfectly with the phrase in the prophecy in Daniel 9:25. The decree contained all that was necessary to restore and to build Jerusalem. (Ref. Ezra 7:11-26, and Nehemiah 2:1-20)

The decree to rebuild the Temple at Jerusalem, which was indeed given by Cyrus and reiterated by Darius, should not be confused with the seventy week prophecy which commenced with the decree by Artexerxes, who did according to the word of the Lord in Daniel 9:25, and that was "commandment to restore and to build Jerusalem". Although the decree to rebuild was given and work started and later stopped for sixteen years, and resumed later, the prophecy came into existence only when Artexerexes gave the decree to restore and rebuild Jerusalem.

THE DURATION OF SEVENTY YEARS

The duration and the distribution of seventy years is mentioned in Daniel 9:26

The Messiah is crucified after 62 weeks of years after the building of Zerubbabel's Temple i.e 62x7= 434 years

And after threescore and two weeks shall Messiah be cut off, but not for himself: and the people of the prince that shall come shall destroy the city and the sanctuary; and the end thereof shall be with a flood, and unto the end of the war desolations are determined. (Daniel 9:26)

THE ACTION IN FINAL SEVEN YEARS

The action in the final week of seven years is mentioned in Daniel 9:27 i.e 1x7=7 years

And he shall confirm the covenant with many for one week: and in the midst of the week he shall cause the sacrifice and the oblation to cease, and for the overspreading of abominations he shall make it desolate, even until the consummation, and that determined shall be poured upon the desolate. (Daniel 9:27)

The end of Seventy weeks is the time when 'ABOMINAITON OF DESOLATION' sets in and thereafter, the LORD returns to the earth. It is when the anointing of the most Holy takes place.

SUM UP THE YEARS

49 YEARS + 434 YEARS + 7 YEARS = 490 YEARS

The 434 period of years is the Church age, also known as the "Grace Period".

Credits: Flavius Joseph, Antiquities of the Jews - Book XI by Public Domain for Cyrus, Darius, Artexerexes

CHAPTER 13 THE IMPRESSIVE INTERLUDE

REVELATION CHAPTER 7 EXPLALINED

The text from Revelation Chapter 7 is posted followed by my exposition. The original text is posted to show that I am not adding anything to the text or removing anything from the text. The explanation that follows is I understand the text.

THE TEXT

Revelation 7:1 And after these things I saw four angels standing on the four corners of the earth, holding the four winds of the earth, that the wind should not blow on the earth, nor on the sea, nor on any tree.

2 And I saw another angel ascending from the east, having the seal of the living God: and he cried with a loud voice to the four angels, to whom it was given to hurt the earth and the sea,

3 Saying, Hurt not the earth, neither the sea, nor the trees, till we have sealed the servants of our God in their foreheads.

4 And I heard the number of them which were sealed: and there were sealed an hundred and forty and four thousand of all the tribes of the children of Israel.

5 Of the tribe of Juda were sealed twelve thousand. Of the tribe of Reuben were sealed twelve thousand. Of the tribe of Gad were sealed twelve thousand.

6 Of the tribe of Aser were sealed twelve thousand. Of the tribe of Nepthalim were sealed twelve thousand. Of the tribe of Manasses were sealed twelve thousand.

7 Of the tribe of Simeon were sealed twelve thousand. Of the tribe of Levi were sealed twelve thousand. Of the tribe of Issachar were sealed twelve thousand.

8 Of the tribe of Zabulon were sealed twelve thousand. Of the tribe of Joseph were sealed twelve thousand. Of the tribe of Benjamin were sealed twelve thousand.

9 After this I beheld, and, lo, a great multitude, which no man could number, of all nations, and kindreds, and people, and tongues, stood before the throne, and before the Lamb, clothed with white robes, and palms in their hands;

Israel and The Church

10 And cried with a loud voice, saying, Salvation to our God which sitteth upon the throne, and unto the Lamb.

11 And all the angels stood round about the throne, and about the elders and the four beasts, and fell before the throne on their faces, and worshipped God,

12 Saying, Amen: Blessing, and glory, and wisdom, and thanksgiving, and honour, and power, and might, be unto our God for ever and ever. Amen.

13 And one of the elders answered, saying unto me, What are these which are arrayed in white robes? and whence came they?

14 And I said unto him, Sir, thou knowest. And he said to me, These are they which came out of great tribulation, and have washed their robes, and made them white in the blood of the Lamb.

15 Therefore are they before the throne of God, and serve him day and night in his temple: and he that sitteth on the throne shall dwell among them.

16 They shall hunger no more, neither thirst any more; neither shall the sun light on them, nor any heat.

17 For the Lamb which is in the midst of the throne shall feed them, and shall lead them unto living fountains of waters: and God shall wipe away all tears from their eyes.

EXPOSITION

Revelation Chapter 7 can be identified as an interlude or break or intermission between Chapter 6 and Chapter 8. (This kind of interlude happens several times in the Book of Revelation – 6, a break and 7 like six angels, a break and seventh, six trumpets, a break and seventh).

This chapter provides us a quest to seek answers to some of our intriguing questions related to the Church, Great Tribulation, The sealing of the twelve tribes, preaching the Gospel during Great Tribulation, the Church reigning with Lord Jesus, and the worshippers in the Temple during Millennium.

Apostle John says, after the things mentioned in Chapter 6 of Revelation had come to pass, he saw four angels standing on the four corners of the earth, holding four winds that they may not hurt the earth, or the sea, or the trees before the appointed time.

Israel and The Church

The four angels were strong enough to hold the winds. The four winds blow from four poles of the earth; the North Pole, the South Pole, the East Pole, and the West Pole. Who can hold the winds except angels at the command of God? Who can direct the paths of the winds except God Himself?

Another angel came from the east and said to the angels not to hurt the earth until the servants of God were sealed in their foreheads. John heard the number of those who were sealed on their foreheads and they were 144,000; twelve thousand from each of the twelve tribes as mentioned in Revelation 7:5-8

A common question that arises in the minds of believers is that will anyone be able to be saved during great tribulation period, and if so, who are those, and how salvation is provided. The reason to ask such question is because of the knowledge that we have that the church will be 'caught up' when Lord Jesus Christ comes again and Holy Spirit, who is the restrainer, is withdrawn from the world.

Holy Spirit, the restrainer, is removed from the earth immediately when the Church is caught up and with the absence of Holy Spirit in the world, the Antichrist is revealed.

"And now ye know that which restrains, that he should be revealed in his own time"(2 Thessalonians 2:6)

Until the Church is 'caught up' the restrainer restrains Antichrist from being revealed and to have any power in the world. This Antichrist is not the one that is referred in 1 John, but he is the 'man of sin' and 'son of perdition'.

The members of the Church have glorified bodies, and will reign with Lord Jesus Christ on those who are saved during the great Tribulation period and thereafter.

"In a moment, in the twinkling of an eye, at the last trump: for the trumpet shall sound, and the dead shall be raised incorruptible, and we shall be changed" (1 Corinthians 15:52)

After the Church is 'caught up' there would be no restrainer in the world, and the evil will be rampant. The Holy Spirit visits the earth on specific individuals just as He was visiting in the Old Testament period.

In this period of interlude the 144,000 of purely Jewish descends from the twelve tribes of Israel, will be sealed unto redemption, and they will be protected from Great Tribulation. They are sealed unto redemption similar to the

Israel and The Church

members of the Church are sealed inasmuch as they accept Jesus as their Savior. They come to be under the Church, where is there is no difference between Jews and Gentiles.

"In whom ye also trusted, after that ye heard the word of truth, the gospel of your salvation: in whom also after that ye believed, ye were sealed with that holy Spirit of promise" (Ephesians 1:13)

The protection they enjoy will be just as the children of Israel were protected from Egyptian plagues.

The 144,000 are those, whose eyes are not blind anymore, but opened to see and believe the truth of the knowledge of the Lord Jesus Christ. They are the ones who enjoy the same privilege as the Church enjoys.

"But their minds were made dull, for to this day the same veil remains when the old covenant is read. It has not been removed, because only in Christ is it taken away. Even to this day when Moses is read, a veil covers their hearts. 16 But whenever anyone turns to the Lord, the veil is taken away" 2 Corinthians 3:14-16.

Did God chose only 144,000 to be sealed during the great tribulation period out of 15 million Jews in the world today? Yes, that is what the text says, and no one is authorized to allegorize to some other number, or say 'Church is spiritual Israel' etc. The Church is the body of Christ and not spiritual Israel. Israel is not the Church. The rest of them are the ones who have refused to accept Jesus as their Messiah, but will acknowledge Him as their Messiah when the 144,000 preach Gospel to the world.

The Bible says every knee shall bow and acknowledge the name of Jesus and the rest of the Jews who are not sealed are no exception to this saying:

"That at the name of Jesus every knee should bow, of things in heaven, and things in earth, and things under the earth" (Philippians 2:10)

The Church in this period will be in heaven with the Lord, and these 144,000 are sealed with the Holy Spirit unto salvation, just as any member of the Church is sealed with the Holy Spirit unto redemption to be conformed to the image of His Son.

The member of the Church does not mean a member of local Church, but the body of Christ, whose head is Lord Jesus Christ. It should be clear by now that the Church is 'caught up' when the Lord comes again with the shout of the archangel at the last trump and the dead in Christ shall rise first and those who are alive at that time will be caught to meet the Lord in the air and be with Him for ever and ever.

"For the Lord himself shall descend from heaven with a shout, with the voice of the archangel, and with the trump of God: and the dead in Christ shall rise first: Then we which are alive and remain shall be caught up together with them in the clouds, to meet the Lord in the air: and so shall we ever be with the Lord" (1 Thessalonians 4:16-17)

Those Jewish descendants numbering 144,000 from the twelve tribes would be on the earth yet they belong to the Church. Those 144,000 will proclaim the Gospel of Jesus Christ to the ends of the earth, and at this time that the promise would be fulfilled that there shall not a single one left on this earth that has not heard the Gospel of Jesus Christ.

After 144,000 were sealed, John saw a great multitude that could not be numbered by any man coming up from all nations, all kindred, all people, and tongues. They all stood before the Lamb. They were all clothed in white robes, and palms in their hands. They cried with loud voice saying "Salvation belongs to our God, who sits on the throne, and to the Lamb."

This multitude of people is the remnant of Jews and Gentiles saved during the Great Tribulation period by the Gospel of Jesus Christ proclaimed by 144,000, and martyred. There is a clear demarcation here and the Church has the members of Christ, and the 144,000 sealed of the Jewish descendants. They do have the glorified bodies and will worship the Lord in heaven. All the 144,000 will all be in the new Heaven.

There is no temple in heaven. This is very firmly affirmed in Revelation 21:22.

And I saw no temple therein: for the Lord God Almighty and the Lamb are the temple of it. (Revelation 21:22)

The temple that is referred to in Revelation Chapter 11:1 is one that would be built during Great Tribulation period. This is evident from the fact that the seventh trumpet was not blown nor seven vials were poured out during the time period mentioned in Revelation Chapter 11:1.

There is mention of 'temple' in Revelation Chapter 11:19. This is the actual abode of God, the Holy of Holies to which there is access for men. John saw the Ark of the Testament of God there and "there came flashes of

Israel and The Church

lightning, rumblings, peals of thunder, an earthquake and a severe hailstorm". Lightning, thunders, and earthquake describe the majesty of God.

"Then God's temple in heaven was opened, and within his temple was seen the ark of his covenant. And there came flashes of lightning, rumblings, peals of thunder, an earthquake and a severe hailstorm". *(Revelation 11:19)*

And I saw no temple therein: for the Lord God Almighty and the Lamb are the temple of it. (Revelation 21:22)

These multitudes, of people that John saw, are those, who would have heard the Gospel of Jesus Christ from the mouths of 144,000 of Jewish redeemed children of God. These multitudes of people do not have the glorified bodies and they will worship the Lord in the temple on the new earth.

One of the elders inquired John if he knew who in white robes were, and where they came from. When John said "Sir, you know", the elder said to him, "These are they who have come out of the great tribulation; they have washed their robes and made them white in the blood of the Lamb".

The elder also explained to John that they are before the throne of God and serve Him day and night in His temple, and He who sits on the throne will dwell among them. Because the LORD is with them they shall neither hunger nor thirst anymore and neither the sun shall light on them nor would they suffer from any heat. The Lamb will feed them and lead them to the living fountains of waters. God will wipe away their tears from their eyes.

My tabernacle also shall be with them: yea, I will be their God, and they shall be my people. (Ezekiel 37:27)

John heard the number of those who were sealed on their foreheads and they were 144,000; twelve thousand from each of the twelve tribes as mentioned in Revelation 7:5-8. Those who were sealed were

From the tribe of Judah 12,000,

From the tribe of Reuben 12,000,

From the tribe of Gad 12,000,

From the tribe of Asher 12,000,

From the tribe of Naphtali 12,000,

From the tribe of Manasseh 12,000,

From the tribe of Simeon 12,000,

From the tribe of Levi 12,000,

From the tribe of Issachar 12,000,

From the tribe of Zebulun 12,000,

Israel and The Church

From the tribe of Joseph 12,000, and

From the tribe of Benjamin are sealed 12,000.

Judah is listed first because Reuben lost his birthright because he defiled the bed of his father, Jacob.

The scepter is given to Judah, and Jesus is called the lion of the tribe of Judah and the scepter of Judah shall not depart from him.

Every one of the angels, who stood around the throne of God, and around the elders, and around the four beasts, fell prostrate on their faces before the throne and worshipped God saying, "Amen: Blessing, and glory, and wisdom, and thanksgiving, and honour, and power, and might, be unto our God for ever and ever. Amen".

TRIBULATION SAINTS

In response to the Gospel message proclaimed by the 144,000 Jews, who were sealed from the twelve tribes of Israel, there was a multitude of people accepted Jesus as the Lord, and John could not number them. They were from every nation, every tribe, and people and languages. They were all standing before the throne and the Lamb. What then, is the difference between the throne and the Lamb? Obviously The Father God was in His throne, still invisible for anyone, and the Lamb of God, who is our Savior, Lord Jesus Christ was by His side.

The multitude, who could not be numbered, cried out in a loud voice saying:

"Salvation belongs to our God,
who sits on the throne,
and to the Lamb"

The angels, who were standing around the throne, and around the elders and four living creatures, fell prostrate down before the throne and worshipped God saying:

"Amen!
Praise and glory
and wisdom and thanks and honor
and power and strength
be to our God for ever and ever.
Amen!"

While the multitude worshipped saying "Salvation belongs to our God, who sits on the throne, and to the Lamb" the angels worshipped God saying: "Amen, praise and glory and wisdom and thanks and honor, and power and strength be to our God for ever and ever. Amen.

Israel and The Church

From among the twenty four elders, who were representatives of the Church, one elder asked John if he recognized those multitudes that were in white robes, and where they came from.

As it was a rhetorical question designed to answer rather than seeking an answer, John said to the elder "Sir, you know". If there were disciples of Jesus or anyone from either Old Testament saints viz. Abraham, Isaac, or Jacob, or New Testament saints, John would have certainly recognized them, but he did not recognize anyone of them; rather he said, "Sir, you know".

The elder answered John that they are the ones who have not obeyed or worshipped Antichrist and come out of great tribulation having become martyrs for Lord Jesus Christ and rose to life.

A very notable fact here is that they are ever before the throne of God and serve Him day and night in His temple. The question is how the temple appeared in heaven. The answer is that the temple is not in new heaven, but is on the new earth, and God is in His holy temple, for them, as promised in Jeremiah 31:33 and Ezekiel Chapter 37:28. God made covenant as follows:

"This is the covenant I will make with the people of Israel after that time," declares the Lord. "I will put my law in their

minds and write it on their hearts. I will be their God, and they will be my people" Jeremiah 31:33*

For New Testament believers it was already fulfilled according to Luke 22:20.

"In the same way, after the supper he took the cup, saying, "This cup is the new covenant in my blood, which is poured out for you".

The multitude that came out from the great tribulation served God in his temple. God will shelter them with His presence, and they never again thirst, not does sun will beat them down and no scorching heat will hurt them. The Lamb at the center of the throne will be their shepherd, and he will lead them to springs of living water, and God will wipe away tears from their eyes.

The prophecy in Isaiah 49:10 will be fulfilled.

"They will neither hunger nor thirst,
 nor will the desert heat or the sun beat down on them.
He who has compassion on them will guide them
 and lead them beside springs of water"

CHAPTER 14 ABOMINATION OF DESOLATION

"When ye therefore shall see the abomination of desolation, spoken of by Daniel the prophet, stand in the holy place, (whoso readeth, let him understand)" (Matthew 24:15)

Lord Jesus Christ spoke of 'abomination of desolation' as the sign to know that the end days are here; and it is time for Him to come again. Prophets in the Old Testament period spoke of the end days, and Lord Jesus Christ reiterated those prophecies, and elaborated vividly about His second coming. The second coming of Lord Jesus Christ is the hope of every believer.

It is the hope of every believer in Christ that when the Lord comes again the dead shall rise from the graves, and those who are alive will be caught up together, to be with Him for ever and ever. After the final seven-year-period is over He along with the believers will step on the earth. For those who did not believe Lord Jesus Christ as their savior it will the beginning of their sorrows of intolerable levels. Those unbelievers, who were already dead by then; they will rise from the graves after the thousand-year-reign of

Second Coming of Jesus

Jesus Christ is over, and they will be judged in order that they may be cast into the 'lake of fire'.

As seen in Matthew 24:15 Lord Jesus quotes Daniel's prophecy and shows how the beginning of the end days will be. The prophecy of the timing of His second coming is in Daniel 9:24-27. While quoting the prophecy and giving His disciples signs that precede His second coming, He said no one knows the timing of His second coming; not even He Himself. The timing of His second coming is known only to the Father.

By the word of Lord Jesus Christ it is clear that all the predictions made by men in the past, and those that will be made in future about His second coming are false and fake.

However, the events triggering the second coming of Lord Jesus Christ are detailed in the Scriptures. Those who can take delight in knowing the details would enjoy the prophecies, and will warn those who have not come to Jesus yet. It is for this purpose that the details are so vividly presented in the Book of Revelation.

Israel and The Church

John saw in his vision the events that have already occurred, the events that are, and the events that will be in future. He saw Antichrist coming up; he saw that there will be 'great tribulation', he saw the vials of wrath being poured out by angels onto the earth, he saw the 'Son of man' coming with His angels, he saw the destruction of Antichrist by the word of the Lord that came from His mouth; he saw the thousand-year-reign of Lord Jesus Christ, he saw the present earth, and present heavens rolling away like the scrolls, he saw the temple, he saw the New Jerusalem coming out of heaven that has no temple in it, and he saw many more details of the 'Kingdom of God'.

It is, therefore, obvious that predictions made by men, in any period of time, about the second coming of Jesus, are false and guess-work. Although the events that happen before His second coming are revealed in the Bible, yet the time of His second coming will be like a thief breaking into a house. God wants us to be alert and to watch for the events that are already recorded for us to read and understand.

"Watch therefore: for ye know not what hour your Lord doth come. But know this, that if the goodman of the house had known in what watch the thief would come, he would have watched, and would not have suffered his house to be broken up" (Matthew 24:42-43)

Bible instructs us not be taken away by false predictions and false date-setters, and even when they say here is Christ or there is Christ

"Then if any man shall say unto you, Lo, here is Christ, or there; believe it not". (Matthew 24:23)

CHAPTER 15 THE ABOMINATION

"When ye therefore shall see the abomination of desolation, spoken of by Daniel the prophet, stand in the holy place, (whoso readeth, let him understand:)" (Matthew 24:15)

Old Testament speaks of 'abomination' of different kinds (cf. Lev 11:42, Lev 18:22, Lev 20:13 and Deut. 7:25). However, in the context that is in reference to the second coming of Lord Jesus, it was about the 'abomination' that was spoken of by Daniel the prophet, and reiterated by the Lord Jesus Christ. The prophecy was:

"And he shall confirm the covenant with many for one week: and in the midst of the week he shall cause the sacrifice and the oblation to cease, and for the overspreading of abominations he shall make it desolate, even until the consummation, and that determined shall be poured upon the desolate" (Daniel 9:27)

The Antichrist confirms the Covenant that God made in Jeremiah 31:31-33 and deceives Israel into believing that He is the real Messiah. The children of Israel will be misled by his confirmation and the temporary peace he brings to them, they indeed believe him to be their savior. In the mid-week i.e. after three and half years of final week of the seventy-week prophecy of Daniel he will break the covenant that he made and will cause the sacrifices and the oblation to cease.

Greek Strong's Number 946 "bdelugma" is translated as "Abomination". This word occurs in Matt 24:15; Mark 13:14; Luke 16:15; Revelation 17:4-5 and Revelation 21:27

John the prophet saw, in his vision as recorded, in the book of Revelation that the woman was full of abominations and filthiness of her fornication and she was carried by the beast which had seven heads and ten horns.

The woman is symbolic expression of idol. Upon her forehead was a name written "MYSTERY, BABYLON THE GREAT, THE MOTHER OF HARLOTS AND ABOMINATIONS OF THE EARTH". Out of the seven dynasties who ruled Israel after Daniel prophesied, five kings died in succession, and one was ruling Israel when John saw vision, and the last one comes in the end days and He is the Antichrist and who was of those seven kings. (cf. Revelation 17:4-14)

Israel and The Church

The beast in Revelation 17:8 is the symbolic representation of none other than Antichrist, whom John saw in his vision. The beast was earlier very powerful, but it was not so when John saw. However, it comes back with great power.

This beast ascended from the bottomless pit and later goes into destruction. Those believers, whose names are written in the book of life from the foundation of the world, will see the destruction of Antichrist. This is the power "that was, and is not, and yet is".

The seat of this woman was the seat of idolatry and persecution. "Kings of the earth have committed fornication with her and the inhabitants of the earth have been made drunk with wine of her fornication".

One of the seven angels, who had seven vials, talked with John and said "Come hither; I will shew unto thee the judgment of the great whore that sitteth upon many waters". (cf. Revelation 17:1-2)

The meaning of the word "waters" is explained in Revelation 17:15. It is the abomination, the idolatry that controlled the "peoples, and multitudes, and nations, and tongues". In the Old Testament period the children of Israel offered sacrifices to other gods, namely, Baal, Ashtharoth, Molech, Chemosh etc.

God said the children of Israel have committed spiritual adultery by worshipping idols; and He hates idolatry. When they took part in the pleasure with idols, they became one with them, and therefore, the LORD used very strong language against them saying:

"And I saw, when for all the causes whereby backsliding Israel committed adultery I had put her away, and given her a bill of divorce; yet her treacherous sister Judah feared not, but went and played the harlot also" (Jeremiah 3:8)

"And they forsook the LORD, and served Baal and Ashtaroth" (Judges 2:13)

"Then did Solomon build an high place for Chemosh, the abomination of Moab, in the hill that is before Jerusalem, and for Molech, the abomination of the children of Ammon" (1 Kings 11:7)

"And they built the high places of Baal, which are in the valley of the son of Hinnom, to cause their sons and their daughters to pass through the fire unto Molech; which I commanded them not, neither came it into my mind, that they should do this abomination, to cause Judah to sin". (Jeremiah 32:35)

"How shall I pardon thee for this? thy children have forsaken me, and sworn by them that are no gods: when I had fed them to the full, they then committed adultery, and assembled themselves by troops in the harlots' houses" (Jeremiah 5:7)

The LORD God gave the command to the children of Israel not to worship idols, and not to have any other gods before Him. God delivered the children of Israel from the bondage of slavery, with His mighty outstretched arm, and while they were on their journey to the Promised Land He warned them with these words.

"The graven images of their gods shall ye burn with fire: thou shalt not desire the silver or gold that is on them, nor take it unto thee, lest thou be snared therein: for it is an abomination to the LORD thy God. Neither shalt thou bring an abomination into thine house, lest thou be a cursed thing like it: but thou shalt utterly detest it, and thou shalt utterly abhor it; for it is a cursed thing" (Deuteronomy 7:25-26)

"Abomination" is that which is 'detestable' and without any doubt it is idolatry. God hated the idolatry of any kind in both the Old Testament period and in the New Testament period. He detested man bowing down to idols and worshipping them. God never tolerated any king or ordinary citizen who had any other god before Him. The Bible says nothing that abominates will enter heaven.

"And there shall in no wise enter into it any thing that defileth, neither whatsoever worketh abomination, or maketh a lie: but they which are written in the Lamb's book of life" (Revelation 21:27)

We cannot but worship the Lord, who created heavens and earth, the seas and all that is therein, and revealed His glory in nature. His throne is heaven and earth is His footstool, and who can confine God in a temple? Worshipping idols, creation and nature instead of worshiping the creator is so hateful to God that He punishes any kind of idol worship. Idol worship is the "abomination".

"When I consider thy heavens, the work of thy fingers, the moon and the stars, which thou hast ordained; What is man, that thou art mindful of him? and the son of man, that thou visitest him? For thou hast made him a little lower than the angels, and hast crowned him with glory and honour" (Psalms 8:3-5)

Israel and The Church

God commands us not to fear because He is with us always; and not to be dismayed because He is our God, who is strength Himself and strengthens and helps us. He promises that He will pour water upon him that is thirsty and floods upon the dry ground. He promises that He will give living water and everlasting life (cf. Isaiah 41:10-11; Isaiah 44:3-4; John 4:10, 11; John 3:16)

CHAPTER 16 THE DESOLATION

Desolation is the ruins caused by the abomination. This word is translated from Greek word "eremos" Greek Strong's Number 2048 and its definition is:

"Of uncertain affinity; lonesome, i.e. (by implication) waste (usually as a noun "chora" Greek Strong's number 5561 being implied):--desert, desolate, solitary, wilderness". It is devastation and that which is 'lay waste'.

During the period of Ezra the scribe, and Nehemiah the cup-bearer of King Ahesuerus, the temple was rebuilt, and it was widely known as "Zerubbabel's temple" after the name of Zerubbabel, son of Shealtiel Governor of Judah, who took much interest in rebuilding the temple. Jeshua, son of Josedech helped him in the construction of the temple much with the encouragement, admonishing of Prophets Haggai and Zechariah.

The first temple which was built by the great king of Israel Solomon, was looted by Shisaq, king of Egypt (1 Kings 14:25-26), and later it was destroyed by King Nebuchadnezzar of Babylon (2 Kings 24:11. 2 Kings 25:9) and all the holy vessels from the temple were carried away to Babylon. Nebuchadnezzar also carried away Jews from the southern kingdom of Israel, which was known as "House of Judah" to Babylon. Daniel was one of the captives taken by Nebuchadnezzar to Babylon.

It may be recalled that Solomon went after the gods of his several wives and did not keep the LORD's statutes and, therefore, God's wrath came upon his kingdom, yet not in his days but during the days of his posterity because God promised to have mercy on Solomon.

"I will be his father, and he shall be my son. If he commit iniquity, I will chasten him with the rod of men, and with the stripes of the children of men: But my mercy shall not depart away from him, as I took it from Saul, whom I put away before thee" (2 Samuel 7:14-15)

Daniel's prophesied in the book of Daniel chapter 11:21-45 about a king who comes and causes abomination and it was fulfilled when "Antipas Epiphanies" king from Syria besieged Jerusalem and persecuted Jews and set up an abomination in their temple.

Flavius Joseph the historian records in his book on "Wars of the Jews Book 1 Chapter 1" about a tyrannous king named Antipas Epiphanes who set up, 'Zeus' a Greek god, in the Zerubbabel's temple. The holy temple of Jews was thus forced to have in it an idol, which was an abomination in the sight of the LORD. Antipas ordered offering of pigs as sacrifice to his god "Zeus" on the altar. He persecuted Jews and stopped their sacrifices and oblation in the temple. He also stopped circumcision and outlawed "Judaism" in 167 B.C. He looted the temple and desecrated it. Antiochus Epiphanies died of a serious disease after his return from eastern expedition.

Zerubbabel's temple was reconstructed by Herod and it was in this Herod's temple that the earthly parents of Jesus offered two turtledoves as sacrifice; and it was this temple where Jesus, later in his ministry, overthrew merchants and their merchandise for desecrating the temple.

Consequent upon Jews calling upon themselves and their children blood of Jesus Christ and demanding His crucifixion God's wrath was poured upon Jerusalem, when Titus the Emperor under Nero destroyed the temple and leveled it and the city Jerusalem to the ground in A.D 70.

Psalmist wrote:

Israel and The Church

"For they provoked him to anger with their high places, and moved him to jealousy with their graven images" (Psalms 78:58)

Israel became virtually non-existent nation and the land was laid waste for many years as a consequence of disobeying the commandments of God and for not keeping His statures. Yet, God said by the word of Hosea the prophet that He will make them one people. By His grace and mercy Israel had regeneration.

As Psalmist sang God's anger does not last long, The LORD brought back the children of Israel, except for those who preferred to stay in their cities in foreign lands, and resurrected the nation as an independent country in 1948. The status-quo at present is that there is a shrine, a holy place, controlled by Islam.

But thou, O Lord, art a God full of compassion, and gracious, longsuffering, and plenteous in mercy and truth. (Psalms 86:15)

CHAPTER 17 ANTICHRIST PART 1

"Let no man deceive you by any means: for that day shall not come, except there come a falling away first, and that man of sin be revealed, the son of perdition" (2 Thessalonians 2:3)

Tribulations and persecutions the believers in Thessalonica suffered in 50-51 A.D were far lesser in intensity than Jews who suffered under Antiochus Epiphanes in 167 B.C.

John writes in 1 John 2:18, 22; Chapter 4:3; and 2 John 1:7 about antichrist, but he was writing about those who deny the Father and the Son.

"Who is a liar but he that denieth that Jesus is the Christ? He is antichrist, that denieth the Father and the Son" (1 John 2:22)

The Antichrist referred to by Lord Jesus Christ is a 'man of sin', who is 'son of perdition' and he is yet to be revealed in this world. Although Antiochus Epiphanes afflicted Jews greatly and outlawed Judaism, yet he did not set up himself as an idol in the temple. He did not command

Israel and The Church

people to worship him and did not show miracles; but he set up 'Zeus' a greek god in the temple.

Jews suffered great persecution under him, and yet it was not 'great tribulation' such as was not seen since the beginning of the world (Ref. Matthew 24:21). Antiochus Epiphanes did not confirm any covenant with Jews of peace or unification of the divided kingdom of Israel.

For then shall be great tribulation, such as was not since the beginning of the world to this time, no, nor ever shall be. (Matthew 24:21)

Antichrist promises peace which Israelites ardently desired and surprisingly he brings in peace temporarily to Israel and affirms that he was the promised Messiah to come. By seeing peace Jews will be totally misled into believing that he was the promised Messiah.

The Messiah had already come into this world in the form of a servant in the likeness of man born of Virgin Mary in a poor family.

"But while he thought on these things, behold, the angel of the Lord appeared unto him in a dream, saying, Joseph, thou son of David, fear not to take unto thee Mary thy wife: for that which is conceived in her is of the Holy Ghost. And she shall bring forth a son, and thou shalt call his name

JESUS: for he shall save his people from their sins" (Matthew 1:20-21)

Jews rejected Jesus as their Messiah inasmuch as their convictions were that the promised Messiah would come like a king. Prophet Isaiah prophesied about seven hundred before Jesus was born as written in Isaiah 9:6-7. The prophecy was literally fulfilled. Jesus came seeking Jews and to restore their kingdom; however, inasmuch as Jews rejected Him and pleaded for his crucifixion, the establishment of the kingdom is postponed. Their rejection of Jesus as their Messiah helped Gentiles to have the privilege to come into the Kingdom of God.

"For unto us a child is born, unto us a son is given: and the government shall be upon his shoulder: and his name shall be called Wonderful, Counsellor, The mighty God, The everlasting Father, The Prince of Peace. Of the increase of his government and peace there shall be no end, upon the throne of David, and upon his kingdom, to order it, and to establish it with judgment and with justice from henceforth even for ever. The zeal of the LORD of hosts will perform this" (Isaiah 9:6-7)

Israel and The Church

Even before Judas Iscariot, one of the twelve disciples of Jesus Christ betrayed him; the LORD knew that he was going to betray Him. While Jesus was praying to the Father for His disciples, He mentioned about Judas Iscariot saying:

"While I was with them in the world, I kept them in thy name: those that thou gavest me I have kept, and none of them is lost, but the son of perdition; that the scripture might be fulfilled" (John 17:12)

Judas Iscariot betrayed Jesus and committed suicide. He would not come back again to life as a 'man of sin' or 'son of perdition' except that he will rise at the end to be judged at the 'great white throne'. The scripture says: "…the dead, small and great, stand before God" and "whosoever was not found written in the book of life" will be cast into the "lake of fire". "The death and hell will be cast into the lake of fire" and this is the second death. (For full verses please read Revelation 20:12-15)

Jesus was crucified, buried and without suffering any corruption of his body he rose from the dead with glorified body and appeared to many. After forty days of His resurrection He ascended into heaven and sent Holy Spirit into this world as He promised to comfort us and dwell in our hearts.

Second Coming of Jesus

Anyone who believes Jesus as the Lord and believe in heart that God raised Him from the death will be saved (Cf. Romans 10:9)

"Blessed and holy is he that hath part in the first resurrection: on such the second death hath no power, but they shall be priests of God and of Christ, and shall reign with him a thousand years" (Revelation 20:6)

Daniel's prophecy says:

"And he shall confirm the covenant with many for one week: and in the midst of the week he shall cause the sacrifice and the oblation to cease, and for the overspreading of abominations he shall make it desolate, even until the consummation, and that determined shall be poured upon the desolate" (Daniel 9:27)

Jesus said:

"When ye therefore shall see the abomination of desolation, spoken of by Daniel the prophet, stand in the holy place, (whoso readeth, let him understand:)" (Matthew 24:15)

Israel and The Church

There is, therefore, one who comes up as mentioned in Revelation Chapter 13, is the Antichrist. In inasmuch as Antiochus Epiphanies did not confirm "with many for one week" before he caused the sacrifices and oblations to cease, and he did not stand in the temple to call himself as God, and also because Judas Iscariot did not set up an abomination in the temple nor did he claim to be God the revealing of Antichrist, 'the man of sin' is yet future.

"And I stood upon the sand of the sea, and saw a beast rise up out of the sea, having seven heads and ten horns, and upon his horns ten crowns, and upon his heads the name of blasphemy" (Revelation 13:1)

CHAPTER 18 JUDAS ISCARIOT BETRAYS

Jesus chose twelve disciples for Him but one of them turned out to be betrayer. After Jesus ended His prayer in Gethsemane, Judas Iscariot, one of the twelve, came along with a great multitude of people, who were sent by chief priests and elders, with swords and staves. Judas Iscariot gave sign to the accompanying multitude that whosoever he kisses was Jesus, and that they could hold him fast.

The prophecy of the betrayal of Jesus, mentioned in the Old Testament, was fulfilled when Judas Iscariot betrayed Him (Ref. Matthew 27:9).

"And I said unto them, If ye think good, give me my price; and if not, forbear. So they weighed for my price thirty pieces of silver. And the LORD said unto me, Cast it unto the potter: a goodly price that I was priced at of them. And I took the thirty pieces of silver, and cast them to the potter in the house of the LORD" (Zechariah 11:12-13)

Israel and The Church

Lord Jesus came into this world in the form of servant and in the likeness of man to redeem mankind from sin, but His price was determined as thirty pieces of silver. When Judas Iscariot received thirty pieces of silver the prophecy in the Old Testament was fulfilled.

Exodus Chapter 21:28-32 contain instructions as to how payment of compensation was to be made if an ox hurts man or woman. If by such hurting a man or woman dies, the ox was to be surely be killed by stoning; and its flesh shall not be eaten. By doing so, the owner of the ox is set free.

However, if the ox pushed a man or woman with its horn, and if the person died, not immediately, but subsequently, the ox was to be stoned to death, and in addition the owner of the ox also was to be put to death.

If a manservant or maidservant was pushed by the ox, the owner of the ox was to give the master of the manservant or maidservant thirty shekels of silver, and the ox was to be stoned. Thus the value of the manservant or maidservant was determined to be thirty pieces of silver. This is how the price of betraying Jesus by Judas Iscariot was determined.

"Who, being in the form of God, thought it not robbery to be equal with God: But made himself of no reputation, and took upon him the form of a servant, and was made in the likeness of men" (Philippians 2:6-7)

God in His providence determined that the thirty pieces of silver used for betrayal of Jesus Christ, by Judas Iscariot, to be used for salvation of Gentiles, when that amount was used for purchase of a land, where dead bodies of Gentiles were buried.

"Then Judas, which had betrayed him, when he saw that he was condemned, repented himself, and brought again the thirty pieces of silver to the chief priests and elders, Saying, I have sinned in that I have betrayed the innocent blood. And they said, What is that to us? see thou to that. And he cast down the pieces of silver in the temple, and departed, and went and hanged himself. And the chief priests took the silver pieces, and said, It is not lawful for to put them into the treasury, because it is the price of blood. And they took counsel, and bought with them the potter's field, to bury strangers in. Wherefore that field was called, The field of blood, unto this day. Then was fulfilled that which was spoken by Jeremy the prophet, saying, And they took the thirty pieces of silver, the price of him that was valued, whom they of the children of Israel did value;

Israel and The Church

And gave them for the potter's field, as the Lord appointed me" (Matthew 27:3-10)

John in his vision saw such provision for Gentiles…

"But the court which is without the temple leave out, and measure it not; for it is given unto the Gentiles: and the holy city shall they tread under foot forty and two months" (Revelation 11:2)

Jews held Gentiles in contempt and allotted the "Potter's field", which was also called "Aceldama", and considered it as the fittest place for burying strangers who came to Jerusalem and died.

"And it was known unto all the dwellers at Jerusalem; insomuch as that field is called in their proper tongue, Aceldama, that is to say, The field of blood" (Acts 1:19)

Judas Iscariot committed suicide as recorded in Acts Chapter 1:15-20 where Peter, the Apostle, declared that the prophecy was fulfilled. Judas Iscariot fell headlong and his bowels gushed out when he burst asunder. Peter's assertion was also based on Psalm 69:26 and Psalm 109:8

CHAPTER 19 ANTICHRIST PART II

"And there appeared another wonder in heaven; and behold a great red dragon, having seven heads and ten horns, and seven crowns upon his heads" (Revelation 12:3)

The activities of Satan are described in Revelation Chapters 12 and 13. God spoke to man and revealed His plans in different ways in different periods of time, to the extent we are supposed to know, not less, not more. He spoke through His prophets in the past and through His Son during the Church age.

The Church was a mystery in the Old Testament period and it was revealed in the New Testament period. Jesus said He will build the Church upon Himself and the gates of Hell shall not prevail against it.

God revealed His plans by dreams to Joseph about the future of his family and him. God revealed His plans to Nebuchadnezzar the king of Babylon about his future and his kingdom and God revealed to John by visions, the past, the present and the future.

Israel and The Church

Ever since the beginning of the creation the two kingdoms that were at war with each other were "the Kingdom of God" and "Kingdom of Satan". Kingdom of God stood always for truth, light, the way, and righteousness. Kingdom of Satan always stood for lies, darkness, the destruction and wickedness.

The Old Dragon that rebelled against God was the Satan who deceived Eve and Adam. They fell from the presence of God because of their transgression of the command of God not to eat of the fruit of the forbidden tree in the Garden of Eden. Thus Satan gained for himself the man, and the earth, and set up his own kingdom. That is the reason why the devil said to Jesus he would give the kingdoms to anyone who worshipped him. Jesus rebuked the devil and said it is written in the Scriptures that no one but God alone should be worshipped.

God cursed Satan for deceiving the man, and He cursed the ground for man, and He said to the woman that she shall bear children in pain.

"And the LORD God said unto the serpent, Because thou hast done this, thou art cursed above all cattle, and above every beast of the field; upon thy belly shalt thou go, and dust shalt thou eat all the days of thy life: And I will put enmity between thee and the woman, and between thy seed and her seed; it shall bruise thy head, and thou shalt bruise his heel" (Genesis 3:14-15)

The enmity between the seed of the woman and the seed of the serpent, started from that point of the history, continued until this day, and will continue until Jesus comes again. Lord Jesus Christ will throw Antichrist the 'son of perdition', and the false prophet into the 'lake of fire' and He will slay, with His sword that proceeds from His mouth, the remnant that followed them; the fowls of the air will eat their flesh (Ref. Revelation 19:20-21).

"And the devil that deceived them was cast into the lake of fire and brimstone, where the beast and the false prophet are, and shall be tormented day and night for ever and ever" (Revelation 20:10)

Apostle Paul refers to the kingdom of Satan in the cosmos system in Ephesians 2:3 and calls the powers in the air as "prince of the power of air" and his "spirit" and as "god of this world" in 2Corinthians 4:4. Apostle John called him as "prince of this world" in John 12:31. Obviously there are unknown numbers of demons in the universe taking charge of the thoughts of human beings and leading them astray from the path of righteousness into wickedness that will eventually end in destruction, which is 'perdition'.

"Wherein in time past ye walked according to the course of this world, according to the prince of the power of the air, the spirit that now worketh in the children of disobedience" (Ephesians 2:2)

The great 'red dragon' referred to in Revelation Chapter 12:3 is the Satan, who controlled seven empires, namely: Egypt, Assyria, Babylon, Persia, Greece, Rome and one that is yet to come is of the Antichrist. The Antichrist regime is yet to be revealed. Antichrist is the 'son of perdition' and perdition means destruction. Satan through Antichrist will lead men into destruction unless they seek the truth and submit to the Lordship of Jesus Christ and believe that He is the 'Son of God', and believe that He died on behalf of us, bearing our sin upon Himself, and was raised from the dead by God.

Apostle Paul exhorts us that we should not fall victim to false preaching that Jesus had already come or His second coming is far away. Those two teachings are false.

The Lord's coming is imminent and He may come anytime now. No one knows when He comes. Everyone needs to be ready to be taken into His Kingdom when He comes; otherwise, the alternative is everlasting damnation and destruction. Lord Jesus Christ is not slack in His promise about His second coming, but He is longsuffering that none of us should be lost but have everlasting life.

"The Lord is not slack concerning his promise, as some men count slackness; but is longsuffering to us-ward, not willing that any should perish, but that all should come to repentance" (2 Peter 3:9)

The Lord shall not come until there is 'falling away' first and then the "man of sin", who is the "son of perdition" is revealed. The "falling away" from faith is departure or defecting from the truth is "Apostasy".

"That ye be not soon shaken in mind, or be troubled, neither by spirit, nor by word, nor by letter as from us, as that the day of Christ is at hand. Let no man deceive you by any means: for that day shall not come, except there come a falling away first, and that man of sin be revealed, the son of perdition" 2 Thessalonians 2:2-3

CHAPTER 20 THE RESTRAINER

"For the mystery of iniquity doth already work: only he who now letteth will let, until he be taken out of the way" (2 Thessalonians 2:7)

There is someone or some power preventing Antichrist to be revealed. This restrainer is not named, yet from the context and from other references it is evident that the restrainer is the Holy Spirit working through the Church.

The Church is still on this earth for the promise of God to be fulfilled that unless the fullness of time is come in, the Church will not be caught up to be with the Lord Jesus Christ. The fullness of time shall be considered as come in when the unknown last Gentile accepts Lord Jesus Christ as his/her personal savior. These facts are known only to the Father; not even the Son.

The Church has unique place in the history. It was a mystery in the Old Testament period and that is the reason why Daniel's prophecy does not contain single word about the Church. The Church is the body of Christ consisting of Jews and Gentiles who received salvation. Lord Jesus Christ is the head of the Church.

Second Coming of Jesus

There are prophecies about the first advent of Jesus in this world, about His sufferings, His death, and His resurrection; but there is not a single prophecy about the establishment of the Church. The mystery of the Church was revealed by Apostle Paul.

"That the Gentiles should be fellow-heirs, and of the same body, and partakers of his promise in Christ by the gospel" (Ephesians 3:6)

Jesus accomplished, on this earth, all things that He came to accomplish according to the will of the Father, and He said to His disciples that He should leave this earth to be with the Father. He promised that He will not leave them comfortless or as orphans but will pray to the Father to send the Holy Spirit, who will testify about Him.

"Nevertheless I tell you the truth; It is expedient for you that I go away: for if I go not away, the Comforter will not come unto you; but if I depart, I will send him unto you" (John 16:7)

Lord Jesus Christ said to His disciples that He would send the "Promise" of His "Father" and commanded them to wait in the city of Jerusalem. He said to them that He will not

Israel and The Church

leave His followers comfortless. He promised it and His promises never fail. As He promised He prayed to the Father to give them another comforter after Him that He may abide with His followers for ever. He also promised that He will come again. After His death, burial and resurrection, He ascended into heaven and now He is seated on the right hand of the Majesty and pleading on behalf of those who received salvation. (Ref. Luke 24:49; John 14:18; John 14:16; Hebrews 1:1-8)

"Ye are all the children of light, and the children of the day: we are not of the night, nor of darkness" (1 Thessalonians 5:5)

Jesus said that the Comforter, who is the Holy Spirit, whom the Father will send in His name, shall teach us, guide us, and convict us of our sins. He will bring to our remembrance all things that the Lord said. The Holy Spirit is the "Spirit of truth" and will testify about Lord Jesus Christ. (Ref. John 14:26; John 15:26)

As seen in Acts 1:4 and Acts 2:33 after Jesus ascended into heaven Holy Spirit came into this world and indwelt His disciples; and He will indwell all those who believe in Lord Jesus Christ as their savior and believe in heart that God raised Him from the dead. All those who receive salvation will be sealed with the promise of Holy Spirit.

Second Coming of Jesus

In whom ye also trusted, after that ye heard the word of truth, the gospel of your salvation: in whom also after that ye believed, ye were sealed with that Holy Spirit of promise (Ephesians 1:13).

Apostle Paul by the revelation of Lord Jesus Christ wrote in his second epistle to Thessalonians that they should not be deceived by any means or by any false preaching that day of the Lord has already come, or He will not come. The day of the Lord shall not come until there is 'apostasy', and 'apostasy' is the departure from the truth. When there is departure from the truth surely there will be wickedness.

Of truth there is already wickedness in this world to a great extent; but the wickedness that Paul was referring to was about the onset of lawlessness. The wickedness during the days of lawlessness will be so much as was never before, nor will there be in future after the Antichrist is thrown into the 'lake of fire'. The world has never seen so great persecution of the left-behind people after the Church is taken away from this world. There will be 'great tribulation' during the regime of the one who would be the lawless ruler, the 'son of perdition', the Antichrist.

Israel and The Church

Unless the Church is caught up to meet the Lord in the air, the Antichrist will not be revealed and the Holy Spirit, who is the restrainer is now preventing such great lawlessness as would come with the 'man of sin', the 'son of perdition', who is the Antichrist. Holy Spirit comforts and protects the children of God from 'great tribulation' because the Church is built by Lord Jesus Christ and, therefore, the gates of hell shall not prevail against the Church.

"And I say also unto thee, That thou art Peter, and upon this rock I will build my church; and the gates of hell shall not prevail against it". (Matthew 16:18)

CHAPTER 21 THE TWO WITNESSES

During the last three-and-half-year period in Daniel's prophetical seventieth week of seven years God sends the two witnesses to bear His testimony and seeks the children of Israel to accept Jesus Christ as their Messiah. (Daniel's one prophetical week is equivalent to seven years). Although they are not identified by their names in the Scriptures, yet the best possible interpretation is that they are Moses and Elijah or two individuals in the spirit of Moses and Elijah, just as John the Baptist was in the spirit of Elijah during the days when Jesus was on this earth. The ministry of the two witnesses will start at the commencement of the 'great tribulation' during the reign of Antichrist.

God gives the two witnesses great power and if any man hurts them fire proceeds from their mouth and consume their enemies and thus will their enemies be killed until their allotted time of prophesying on this earth, before Lord Jesus Christ is revealed on this earth

A tyrannous king Antichrist, the 'man of sin' who would have been already on the soil of Israel from the beginning

Israel and The Church

of Daniel's prophetical seventieth week of final seven years will break his confirmed covenant at midpoint, i.e. after three and half years of his reign and persecutes the children of Israel to suffer the 'great tribulation' such as was never before from the midpoint of his reign till the next three and half years.

It is at this time that the two witnesses come onto the scene to defy Antichrist and bear witness of the Promised Messiah. These two witnesses are called " two olive trees and the two candlesticks" standing before the God of the earth" (Rev. 11:4).

The 144,000 of the sons of Israel, twelve thousand from each of the twelve tribes of the sons of Jacob, who were sealed by God unto redemption, as detailed in Revelation Chapter 7, will bear testimony about Lord Jesus before Jews first, and then before others.

The two witnesses are given the power to shut heaven and cause it not to rain during the days of prophecy, similar to the holding up of rain for three and half years by Elijah. They have the power to turn the waters into blood just as Moses and Aaron turned the water into blood when Pharaoh refused to let the children of Israel go from slavery under him. They can also smite the earth with all plagues, as often as they would like to

Those who accept their preaching will in turn bear witness of Lord Jesus Christ to the remnant and thus many Jews will call upon God to save them from the 'great tribulation'.

God will protect the children of Israel who call upon God for help. There will be many who refuse Jesus as their Messiah even under great persecution by the Antichrist. It is beyond comprehension that those who reject Lord Jesus Christ as their Messiah will worship the Antichrist, the "man of sin". They rejected the 'Son of God' when He came first as the 'Lamb of God' to save them from their sins and restore their Kingdom.

Surprisingly even when they are under 'great tribulation' they prefer to worship a man rather the 'Son of God'. The testimony of Jesus is the prophecy and they reject the prophecy of the two witnesses, the 144,000. Those who have called upon Lord Jesus Christ to help them will be protected for a season of time, times and half i.e. three and half years and they are the final nation of Israel consisting of the children of Israel who accept Jesus as their Messiah and thus they are saved individually and as a Nation. It is about them that Apostle Paul wrote that all Israel shall be saved.

Israel and The Church

"And so all Israel shall be saved: as it is written, There shall come out of Sion the Deliverer, and shall turn away ungodliness from Jacob" (Romans 11:26)

As it is evident from the lives of God's servants who work for Him, every servant of God has a definite time limit determined by God to serve Him on this earth. After the lapse of the determined period set by God they will be removed by God from the scene and another servant of God will take his place.

Stephen did not do much work, yet the testimony he bore about Jesus Christ before the high priest was so powerful and immediately after finishing his allotted time he was called by God to be in glory with Him (Ref. Acts chapter 7)

It is not right to think that someone's span of service to God has ended too quickly, because God removed him from this earth. God removes his servant from His service only after the latter has accomplished that which God was allotted to him to perform.

Sometimes the servants of God chose by their own actions to cut short their service to God and express inability, which results in God parting away their portion of blessings from them and give to others. It happened in the lives of most known persons in the Bible and they are Moses and Elijah. Moses said to the LORD that he was not eloquent, slow of speech and tongue. In spite of God promising him that He would be his mouth, yet Moses was reluctant to take up the responsibility assigned to him

God asked him a shrewd question:

"And the LORD said unto him, Who hath made man's mouth? or who maketh the dumb, or deaf, or the seeing, or the blind? have not I the LORD?" (Exodus 4:11)

When Moses continued to show his reluctance, God gave him Aaron his brother to help him and thus he had to share his blessings with Aaron.

And the anger of the LORD was kindled against Moses, and he said, Is not Aaron the Levite thy brother? I know that he can speak well. And also, behold, he cometh forth to meet thee: and when he seeth thee, he will be glad in his heart. (Exodus 4:14)

Elijah by his own saying that he was alone left behind in Israel to work for the Lord resulted in shortening of his career. The Lord said to Elijah that He had reserved for Himself seven thousand men, who did not bow their knees to Baal (Ref. 1 Kings 19:10, 19:18)

Israel and The Church

Likewise, the life span of the two witnesses and their service comes to an end very quickly after Antichrist is revealed. Antichrist will wage a war against the two witnesses and will be triumphant over them and kill them.

"And when they shall have finished their testimony, the beast that ascendeth out of the bottomless pit shall make war against them, and shall overcome them, and kill them" Rev 11:7

The dead bodies of the two witnesses will lie "in the street of the great city, which spiritually is called Sodom and Egypt, where also our Lord was crucified." (Ref. Rev 7:8)

All the people of different languages and nations will see their dead bodies for three and half days and will help their dead bodies to be buried. They who live on the earth during that period will rejoice because the two witnesses tormented them.

To everyone's surprise the two witnesses will rise from their graves after three and half days and all those who see them live again will fear greatly. They hear great voice from heaven saying unto them "come up hither" and on hearing that voice they ascend up to heaven in a cloud and their enemies see them and will be wonderstruck. In the same hour there will be a great earthquake causing tenth part of the city to collapse and seven thousand men will die. The remaining people will fear and give glory to the Lord.

The resurrection of the two witnesses and their ascension is evidence of the power of God to raise all the believers in Christ from the dead. Lord Jesus Christ rose from the dead with glorified body and ascended into heaven and, therefore, He was called the 'first-fruits'. The two witnesses die as martyrs but after three and half days they rise from the dead.

Resurrection is the core belief on which Christianity stands. If there is no resurrection of souls with glorified bodies, then there is absolutely no hope for Christians. They are just as any other man who does not believe in resurrection.

Bible speaks vehemently about life after death and believers' future life with Lord Jesus Christ. We, who have received salvation, will see the Lord face to face and will be confirmed to His image; but for those who do not believe in Lord Jesus Christ the death is cessation of life; the body, brain, mind and soul are fully dead. That is one of the reasons why some people hanker after wealth, fortune, worldly pleasures when they are in this world. For them "there is only one life and 'live out life' with pleasure".

Israel and The Church

They struggle day in and day out to satisfy their fleshly desires and leave their souls to perish eternally.

By raising Lazarus to life Lord Jesus Christ showed that God has the power to raise believers to life. Old Testament saints knew about resurrection. Abraham did not hesitate to obey the Lord when the latter said to him to offer his only promised seed on the altar believing that God will raise him.

"By faith Abraham, when he was tried, offered up Isaac: and he that had received the promises offered up his only begotten son, Of whom it was said, That in Isaac shall thy seed be called: Accounting that God was able to raise him up, even from the dead; from whence also he received him in a figure" (Hebrews 11:17-19)

Job knew that he will rise from the dead.

"For I know that my redeemer liveth, and that he shall stand at the latter day upon the earth" (Job 19:25)

Prophet Isaiah prophecies about resurrection:

"Thy dead men shall live, together with my dead body shall they arise. Awake and sing, ye that dwell in dust: for thy dew is as the dew of herbs, and the earth shall cast out the dead" (Isaiah 26:19)

Second Coming of Jesus

Daniel spoke of dead coming to life

"And many of them that sleep in the dust of the earth shall awake, some to everlasting life, and some to shame and everlasting contempt" (Daniel 12:2)

David spoke of the resurrection of Jesus and all the righteous ones.

"For thou wilt not leave my soul in hell; neither wilt thou suffer thine Holy One to see corruption" (Psalms 16:10)

Of all the promises, comfort and hope that we have in the Bible the most important promise, comfort and hope we have in the words of Apostle Paul. He writes:

"For the Lord himself shall descend from heaven with a shout, with the voice of the archangel, and with the trump of God: and the dead in Christ shall rise first: Then we which are alive and remain shall be caught up together with them in the clouds, to meet the Lord in the air: and so shall we ever be with the Lord" (1 Thessalonians 4:16-17)

"For whom he did foreknow, he also did predestinate to be conformed to the image of his Son, that he might be the firstborn among many brethren" (Romans 8:29)

Israel and The Church

John writes about resurrection:

"But the rest of the dead lived not again until the thousand years were finished. This is the first resurrection. Blessed and holy is he that hath part in the first resurrection: on such the second death hath no power, but they shall be priests of God and of Christ, and shall reign with him a thousand years". (Revelation 20:5-6)

CHAPTER 22 THE LORD IS MIGHTY

"Give unto the LORD, O ye mighty, give unto the LORD glory and strength. Give unto the LORD the glory due unto his name; worship the LORD in the beauty of holiness" (Psalms 29:1-2)

David found grace in the sight of the LORD and calls mighty men of valor to come unto the LORD and give glory due unto His name, and to worship Him in the beauty of His Holiness.

God spoke to His servants in different ways in different times; sometimes in thunder, and sometimes in small still voice. He spoke from the burning bush to Moses, His servant. He spoke from the mercy seat to the High Priest in the Tabernacle, and in small still voice to Elijah, the prophet. God spoke by the mouth of Prophets namely Jeremiah, Isaiah, and many more, and in the last days He spoke through His one and only Son, Lord Jesus Christ. The LORD's voice was upon the waters, His glory was in the thunders, and His voice was powerful.

Israel and The Church

King David says, the LORD's voice and His word were mightier than any sword, or any other weaponry, used by humans to win a battle. There are many incidences in the Word of God, which show that God's word was enough to defeat His enemies. His word is two-edged sword and His right arm is mightier than any weapon, men may use.

"O sing unto the LORD a new song; for he hath done marvellous things: his right hand, and his holy arm, hath gotten him the victory" (Psalms 98:1)

Who can control or direct the thunders, storms and winds from heaven, except for the LORD Himself who causes them at His will, and halts them with His voice at His command. His voice was enough to rattle the strong and elegant cedar trees of Lebanon, and to make Mt. Hermon to dance like a young unicorn. He is mightier than mighty kings. He gave strength to Moses, His servant, to kill Og, king of Bashan, and caused a small stone from the sling of David, His servant, to bring down the giant Goliath to earth, and kill him.

The LORD shook the wilderness of Kadesh and His voice divided the flames of fire. The LORD is the creator and He is the king over all creation. No man can control the natural calamities, except face them with sorrow, and reconstruct their damaged properties, when God brings them on His enemies to punish.

The LORD causes vapors to rise and ascend from the ends of the earth, and brings rain from His treasuries, without any restraint, onto the earth, where His people honor Him. God helps those who seek His help in times of trouble. He never forsakes His people, nor will He fail them, but will always go before them, ever infusing courage and confidence in them to fight the evil.

When Jehoshaphat, king of Judah, the son of Asa, was afraid as the children of Moab, the children of Ammon, and Ammonites went against him in battle. Jehoshaphat went and stood in the house of the LORD and cried to the LORD saying "...O LORD God of our fathers, art not thou God in heaven? and rulest not thou over all the kingdoms of the heathen? and in thine hand is there not power and might, so that none is able to withstand thee? Art not thou our God, who didst drive out the inhabitants of this land before thy people Israel, and gavest it to the seed of Abraham thy friend for ever?" (2 Chronicles 20:5-7)

The Spirit of the LORD came upon Jahaziel, a Levite, a descendant of the sons of Asaph, and he said "Thus saith

Israel and The Church

the LORD unto you, Be not afraid nor dismayed by reason of this great multitude; for the battle is not yours, but God's."

The Levite said to Jehoshaphat that he does not need to fight the battle, but stand still and see the salvation of the LORD. Jehoshaphat bowed his head, and the entire congregation of Judah and the inhabitants of Jerusalem fell before the LORD, and worshipped Him. Jehoshaphat said to all of them to believe in the LORD and then appointed singers unto the LORD and they went forth before the army singing "Praise the LORD; for his mercy endures for ever"

When they sang praises to the LORD, He smote the children of Ammon, Moab and all those who came against Jehoshaphat, king of Judah. The LORD humbled the Amorites, Moabites and Ammonites, the enemies of David (cf. 2 Chronicles 20:1-22)

"Give thanks to the Lord, for he is good, for his steadfast love endures forever. Give thanks to the God of gods, for his steadfast love endures forever. Give thanks to the Lord of lords, for his steadfast love endures forever" (ESV) Psalm 136: 1-3

CHAPTER 23 VESTURE DIPPED IN BLOOD

"And he saith unto me, Write, Blessed [are] they which are called unto the marriage supper of the Lamb. And he saith unto me, These are the true sayings of God" Revelation 19:9

Isaiah prophesied as to how the Lord will trample over his enemies as treading the winepress and will defeat His enemies. The prophecy is yet to be fulfilled. Lord Jesus Christ will defeat Edomites according to the prophecy in Isaiah 63:1-5 and with dyed garments from Bozrah after trampling and treading on them. He is great and mighty in power in His fury He will trample them in fury and He will have the blood sprinkled on his garments. It is His day of taking vengeance upon them. He is righteous and His judgments are true and just.

Bozrah was a chief city in Edom where Edomites, descendants of Esau lived. Bozrah is destroyed and is no more there but the city will rise up in the end days it remains mystery now what the role of this city would be in the days.

Israel and The Church

In reply to the question from Prophet Isaiah, the Lord says that He will tread them in His anger trampling them in His fury, and their blood shall be sprinkled upon His garments. Lord Jesus has already defeated Satan at the cross in order to make a way for our salvation.

"Wherefore art thou red in thine apparel, and thy garments like him that treadeth in the winefat? I have trodden the winepress alone; and of the people there was none with me: for I will tread them in mine anger, and trample them in my fury; and their blood shall be sprinkled upon my garments, and I will stain all my raiment" (Isaiah 63:2-3)

John the Baptist identified Jesus as the "Lamb of God who takes away the sin of the world" (John 1:29). The children of Israel set aside the Passover Lamb on the tenth day of the first month of Jewish calendar i.e. the month of "Abib" and they slew it on fourteenth day of the month (Ref. Exodus 12:1-6). They applied the blood of the lamb to the lintel posts of the doors of their houses in order that the Lord may Passover that home without killing the first born in the house.

The firstborn of the Egyptians including that of Pharaoh was killed by the Lord and then Pharaoh released the children of Israel from the bondage of slavery.

Second Coming of Jesus

"And it came to pass, that at midnight the LORD smote all the firstborn in the land of Egypt, from the firstborn of Pharaoh that sat on his throne unto the firstborn of the captive that was in the dungeon; and all the firstborn of cattle" (Exodus 12:29)

The typology of the slaying of the Lamb for the redemption of the children of Israel from the bondage of slavery is fulfilled when Lord Jesus Christ was crucified on the cross of Calvary for the redemption of mankind. Whoever believes in Jesus as Savior will have salvation free of cost and whoever rejects Him as savior will perish according to John 3:16

Apostle John saw in his vision as recorded in Revelation Chapter 19:13 that Lord Jesus Christ was clothed with vesture dipped in blood.

"And he [was] clothed with vesture dipped in blood: and his name is called The Word of God" Revelation 19:13 and His name was "The Word of God".

"In the beginning was the Word, and the Word was with God, and the Word was God". (John 1:1)

The Word was made flesh and lived among us.

Israel and The Church

"And the Word was made flesh, and dwelt among us, (and we beheld his glory, the glory as of the only begotten of the Father,) full of grace and truth" (John 1:14)

Thus we see three important truths about Lord Jesus Christ.

HE IS THE LAMB OF GOD

HIS VESTURE DIPPED IN BLOOD

HIS NAME IS THE WORD OF GOD

Lord Jesus Christ purchased mediatory power by shedding His own blood. He purchased the blood of His enemies over whom He prevailed by shedding His own blood. He defeated Satan at the cross and His name is the Word of God. God called things into existence and heavens and the earth and all that is therein are created by Him.

God created great whales and everything that moves in the waters. Lastly God created man in His own image after His likeness to have dominion over the fish of the sea, over the fowl of the air and over the cattle and over all the earth and every creeping thing that creeps on the earth.

The LORD God did all this by His word and His word brought everything into existence. His word is double-edged sword and by His word He will smite the nations and rule them with a rod of iron. He treads the winepress of fierceness and the wrath of Almighty God.

Lord Jesus stood before Herod, who was an Edomite, a descendant of Esau, and was mocked at. Herod ridiculed Lord Jesus Christ and sent Him back to Pilate. Pilate excused himself from rendering justice even though he knew that Lord Jesus Christ was innocent and then all the people answered Pilate and said "…His blood be on us, and on our children" (Matthew 27:25).

How could these two mortals escape from being punished for showing injustice to the Lord Jesus Christ? On the day of crucifixion of Lord Jesus Christ Herod and Pilate, who were enemies to each other became friends. The words of Jews and others inviting the curse of the blood of the Lord Jesus Christ were given unto them as gift when Titus came and destroyed Jerusalem in AD 70 and killed Jews and crucified several of them upside down on the walls of Jerusalem. But, the justice to the Edomites that includes Herod is yet future.

The soldiers of the governor showed divine purpose in stripping Jesus and putting on Him a scarlet robe.

Israel and The Church

"And they stripped him, and put on him a scarlet robe" Matthew 27:28

The Blood of Lord Jesus Christ shed on the cross achieved multiple purposes. He defeated Satan at the cross of Calvary. He purchased us with His precious blood and we are saved not with gold or silver but in His blood by grace through faith. He purchased mediatory power and we have access to the Most Holy Place now. He purchased the power to defeat His enemies by shedding His blood on the cross and His name is the Word of God.

The armies, who are the born-again children of God will be clothed in linen, white and clean, and they follow Him from heaven and a sharp sword goes from His mouth and that word will smite the nations. He will rule the nations with rod of iron. He treads "the winepress and wrath of Almighty God" and His vesture and on His thigh a name will be seen and the name is:

"KING OF KINGS, AND LORD OF LORDS"

(Ref: Revelation 19:13-16)

Tell the story of Redemption to the nations. It is the desire of God.

"And it shall be when thy son asketh thee in time to come, saying, What is this? that thou shalt say unto him, By

strength of hand the LORD brought us out from Egypt, from the house of bondage" (Exodus 13:14)

Israel and The Church

CHAPTER 24 ARMAGEDDON WAR

God showed to John in visions the things that should come to pass and all prophecies about the second coming of Lord Jesus Christ will be literally fulfilled. Scriptures affirm that Heaven and earth may fail but the Lord's sayings will never fail.

"For verily I say unto you, Till heaven and earth pass, one jot or one tittle shall in no wise pass from the law, till all be fulfilled" (Matthew 5:18)

It was time for fowls of the air to be present as guests at the marriage supper, of the Lord Jesus Christ and His bride the Church, and have sumptuous meal by eating and being filled with the flesh of the enemies of the Lord.

"And he gathered them together into a place called in the Hebrew tongue Armageddon" (Revelation 16:16)

"Armageddon" is the "the mount of Megiddo", where the final battle between Lord Jesus Christ, and Antichrist and his armies, will take place. "Megiddo" is the venue for many battles that were fought as recorded in the Old Testament vide references Joshua 12:21; 17:11; Judges 1:27; 5:19; 1Kings 4:12; 9:15; 2Kings 9:27; 23:29-30; 1Chronicles 7:29; 2Chronicles 35:22.

The dragon, which is Satan, gave power to the beast, which is Antichrist. Satan deceived men to worship the beast. Men were deceived and worshipped the beast and said "Who is like unto the beast? who is able to make war with him?". Satan gave power to Antichrist to speak blasphemy for forty two months and Antichrist opened his mouth in blasphemy against God, to blaspheme his name, and his tabernacle, and them that dwell in heaven". Antichrist was given power to wage war against the saints and to overcome them and "power was given him over all kindreds, and tongues, and nations" (Ref. Revelation 13:5-8).

After the destruction of religious Babylon by God, John heard a great voice of all the saved righteous believers praising God in heaven saying "Hallelujah: the salvation and the glory and the power of our God" (Ref. Revelation 19:1)

John heard the deafening sound, (somewhat similar to "Niagara falls"), when the servants of God said "Praise our God" and the sound was like rushing waters and thunders. They praised God loudly saying "Hallelujah, for [the] Lord our God the Almighty has taken to himself kingly power".

Israel and The Church

As the Lord Jesus Christ sat upon white horse and rode followed by His army the children of God praised again saying "Hallelujah".

"And I saw heaven opened, and behold a white horse; and he that sat upon him was called Faithful and True, and in righteousness he doth judge and make war" (Revelation 19:11)

Antichrist and the kings of the earth with their armies gathered to wage war against the Lord Jesus Christ.

The Lord's judgments are true and righteous and He "has judged the great harlot which corrupted the earth with her fornication, and has avenged the blood of his bondmen at her hand"

The redeemed saints were joyous and said to one to another encouraging rejoicing and being glad. They gave honor to the Lord because it was time for the marriage of the Lamb to take place. The Lamb is the Lord Jesus Christ (John pointed to Jesus as written in John 1:29, and said "…Behold the Lamb of God, who takes away the sin of the world").

The Church is the Lord's bride (Ref. Ephesians 5:25). She made herself ready to be united in the oncoming "Kingdom of God". God gave the bride (the Church) clean white fine linen to be arrayed in because God considered the fine linen is a sure representation of the righteousness of saints.

John saw an angel standing in the sun calling out loudly the fowl in the air flying in the midst of heaven to come and gather unto the supper of the great God that they "may eat the flesh of kings, and the flesh of captains, and the flesh of mighty men, and the flesh of horses, and of them that sit on them, and the flesh of all men, both free and bond, both small and great".

The angel said to John to write that blessed are those who were called to participate in the marriage supper of the bridegroom and the bride which was to take place on this earth. The Lord affirmed that His sayings are His true sayings, never to fail, never to be questioned, or doubted.

John fell and worshipped the angel who came to speak to him and the angel promptly said to him that he was fellow-servant of him and his brethren. The angel admonished that only God deserves worship and none else, and affirmed that the testimony of Lord Jesus was the spirit of prophecy.

Israel and The Church

As the angel continued speaking John saw heavens opening up and a white horse and He who was riding the horse. The one who sat upon the horse was called "Faithful and True, and in righteousness he doth judge and make war".

The eyes of the one who sat on the white horse were as a flame of fire and he had many crowns. He had a name written and it was not known to anyone except for Himself. His name was "The Word of God" and he was clothed with a vesture of blood indicating his victory over Satan.

The saints in heaven were as armies "clothed in fine linen, white and clean" followed the rider of the white horse from whose mouth a sharp sword went out which smote the nations. He rules the nations with rod of iron and treads "the winepress of the fierceness and wrath of Almighty God".

On the vesture of the rider of the horse was found a name written," KING OF KINGS, AND LORD OF LORDS".

The supposed great mighty battle that was to take place at Armageddon ended surprisingly with a simple word that proceeded from the Lord as John saw in his vision. It was so easy for the Lord to take Antichrist and the false prophet and cast them alive into a "lake of fire burning with brimstone".

Second Coming of Jesus

Smoke rose up for ever and ever indicating the utter defeat of Satan. The twenty four elders representing the Church and the beasts representing the strength, wisdom, etc. fell down and worshipped saying "Amen; Hallelujah" to God who sat on the throne.

The Lord killed the remaining ones with His sword that went forth out of His mouth, and all the fowls had sumptuous marriage supper when they ate and were filled with the flesh of the enemies of the Lord.

Israel and The Church

CHAPTER 25 THE FIVE JUDGMENTS

The following five judgments are seen in the Scriptures:

(1) The Judgment at the cross (John 5:24)

(2) The Judgment in the mid-air for distribution of rewards for saints: (Also called as 'Bema seat of Christ'. (2 Cor. 5:10)

(3) The judgment of Jews and left-behind (Great Tribulation- Matt 24:20-21

(4) The judgment of nations (also known as 'The Sheep and Goat Judgment Matthew 25:40)

(5) The Judgment of the Wicked (Revelation 20:14)

THE JUDGMENT AT THE CROSS

Verily, verily, I say unto you, He that heareth my word, and believeth on him that sent me, hath everlasting life, and shall not come into condemnation; but is passed from death unto life (John 5:24)

It all started with Adam and Eve committing sin in the Garden of Eden, when they both ate the forbidden fruit and bringing sin not only on them, but also on the entire humanity. After the creation is ended 'God planted a garden eastward in Eden; and there he put the man whom he had formed'. (Genesis 2:8)

The first desire from God was that Adam should dress Garden of Eden and keep it, and then God commanded him that he is permitted to eat freely from every fruit, but he shall not eat of the tree of the knowledge of good and evil.

The punishment God detailed for violating his command was that in the day that he eats from the tree of the knowledge of good and evil, he shall surely die. God said that it is not good that the man should be alone; therefore he decided to give him a help met for him. God caused a deep sleep to fall upon Adam, and while he was asleep God took one of the ribs and closed up the flesh. This is the first sleep that God caused upon man in his divine power. That sleep was different from the sleep man would have every night.

It was the deep sleep that God caused upon man. When Adam rose from that deep sleep he saw that the Lord gave him a woman as help mate. God had made Woman from the rib that He took it out of the man. When the woman was brought to the Adam, he called her

Israel and The Church

Woman. They were both naked. As they lived happily the serpent tricked Woman to yield to the temptation on false hopes, and the Woman saw that 'the tree was good for food and pleasant to the eyes'. The Woman took the fruit from the tree and not only she ate it, but she also gave it to her husband and he ate it too. They saw that they were naked and 'they sewed fig leaves together, and made themselves aprons'.

Later on God questioned them and punished them when each of them tried to blame the other. God made coats of skins and clothed Adam and his wife and sent them away from the Garden of Eden. @ Adam called his wife, Eve, because she was the mother of all living.

The sin that these two brought into the world was not such an easy one to be wiped out unless Jesus the Son of God came into this world and took upon Himself the sin of the world, that whosoever believes in him shall be saved.

The curse of 'death' that Adam had reaped upon himself and the whole humanity can be overcome only with the belief in Jesus as one's personal savior. Jesus said that whoever hears his word, and believes on him that sent him, has everlasting life and will not come into condemnation but will pass from death unto life. This is the first judgment when the sin is judged upon the cross and redemption is made available for man.

(2) THE JUDGMENT SEAT OF CHRIST

For we must all appear before the judgment seat of Christ; that every one may receive the things done in his body, according to that he hath done, whether it be good or bad. (2 Corinthians 5:10)

Every believer has to account for the deeds he has done on this earth in order to receive the rewards at the 'Bema seat of Christ' He shall stand at the judgment seat of Christ also known as 'Bema Seat of Christ' not as an unbeliever to receive judgment for punishment, but for rewards he is entitled for working for the Lord.

During the period of time when the believer is with the Lord and after the rapture, the Lord will honor his servants for the service they rendered unto Him when they were on this earth. We are not to judge our brothers because we shall all stand before the judgment seat of Christ (Rom.14:10). The time will come when the Lord comes and He brings to the light every hidden things of darkness, and will show the counsels that have taken place in the hearts.

Israel and The Church

While God does this in the presence of every believer at the judgment seat of Christ every man will praise God (1 Cor.4:5)

Lord Jesus Christ is our life and He will appear in the clouds in glory to receive His own unto Himself and honor them with rewards. It is not the Great white Throne judgment, when those, who have not believed in Him, will be judged for their everlasting destiny in the lake of fire along with the Satan and his angels, but the judgment seat of Christ is the raised seat where He sits as the King of kings to administer justice.

There shall be no condemnation for the believers, who are in Christ, and who have not walked after the flesh, but sought to walk after the Spirit. (Rom 8:1). God was in Christ and reconciled us unto Himself, and made us, who have trusted in Him, and confessed our sins to Him, as his heirs and did not impute our trespasses unto us, but washed our sins in the precious blood of Jesus. We are His workmanship, created in Christ unto good works and we stand worthy of our calling and deserve our rewards at the 'Bema Seat of Christ'.

It is a blessed hope for believer that he will be honored for putting on Christ and for living holy life. It is at this time, when we, the believers are with the Lord, that we will be rewarded before He reveals Himself on this earth again.

(3) GREAT TRIBULATION

Caught in their disbelief Jews have always been waiting for Messiah to come from an earthly King's family. This disbelief in the Messiah, who was their real King, has led them to reject Lord Jesus Christ, the Messiah, as their Savior. Just as a hen gathers her chicken under her wings, God yearned to gather the children of Israel, the blessed generation through, Jesus, who was born in their clan, of the virgin Mary from the lineage of King David, but they not only rejected Him, but also killed prophets and stoned them, who were sent to them.

They rejected the true Messiah, Lord Jesus Christ even to the extent that Jesus, who answered a woman that He was sent unto the lost sheep of Israel was not received by them. But, when the woman, a gentile, who was praying that her daughter be healed by Him, crying, "O Lord, thou Son of David; my daughter is grievously vexed with a devil." (Matt 15:22), and had faith in Him saying, "Truth, Lord: yet the dogs eat of the crumbs which fall from their masters' table". (Matt 15:27), Jesus had compassion on

Israel and The Church

her and granted answer to her prayer. A gentile received because Jews rejected Him.

Apostle Paul writes about this mystery that is revealed in the New Testament about God accepting Gentiles in to the Church. (Ephesians 3:3-9). The Church consisting of individual members, who have accepted Jesus as their Savior, are therefore, given the privilege over the Jews, and they are 'caught up' when the Lord himself 'shall descend from heaven with a shout, with the voice of the archangel, and with the trump of God: and the dead in Christ shall rise first: Then we which are alive and remain shall be caught up together with them in the clouds, to meet the Lord in the air: and so shall we ever be with the Lord'. (1 Thessalonians 4:16-17).

The unbelieving Jews and all others, who have not accepted Jesus Christ as their personal Savior will enter into the 70th week of Daniel, as prophesied in Daniel 9:26,27. Those, who are saved, will be with the Lord, when all others, who are not saved that includes the Jews will left- behind to be under the reign of Antichrist. While the believers are happy with the Lord, and receive their rewards for their good works done on the earth, the unbelievers will be under the reign of Antichrist, who promises them earthly peace, pomp, honor, and wealth.

In the middle of the last week (70th week), that is after completion of 3.5 years, their king, the Antichrist, will break the covenant that he made with them, and then will start the 'great tribulation'. It is at this time that the Jews as prophesied will call upon God to have mercy on them, and God will come their rescue, and every one of them will be saved. Immediately after the tribulation of those days 'great tribulation' are over, 'the sun shall be darkened, and the moon shall not give her light, and the stars shall fall away from heaven and the powers of the heavens shall be shaken'. (Matthew 24:29).

(4)THE JUDGMENT OF NATIONS

The judgment of nations is distinct from the 'Great White Throne Judgment. The nations are the living ones that survive through the 'great tribulation' period, when the gentiles, who are left-behind are judged. This is a period after the Church consisting of believers are 'caught up' to be with the Lord for ever and ever.

In Matthew 5:31-46 there is a description of the judgment that takes place after Lord Jesus Christ reveals himself at His second coming to every one upon this earth. These are the ones, who missed the blessings of being 'caught up' to

Israel and The Church

be with the Lord Jesus for ever and ever, when He comes with the trump of God.

When the believers are 'caught up' to be with the Lord, the dead shall be raised incorruptible and shall be changed in a moment in the twinkling of an eye. Then those, who have put on Christ shall be 'caught up' together with them in the clouds to meet the Lord in the air and they will all be with the Lord for ever and ever. Those, who did not believe in Jesus and did not accept Him as their personal Savior miss these blessings of being 'caught up' and remain on this earth. The dead in sins will remain in their graves and the living will see with their eyes the Lord Jesus revealing Himself upon this earth. The 'Son of man' will come with all the holy angels with him and shall sit upon the throne of glory. This the prophesy proclaimed in Zechariah 14th Chapter.

"And his feet shall stand in that day upon the mount of Olives, which is before Jerusalem on the east, and the mount of Olives shall cleave in the midst thereof toward the east and toward the west, and there shall be a very great valley; and half of the mountain shall remove toward the north, and half of it toward the south". (Zechariah 14:4)

All nations (gentiles) will be gathered unto the Lord Jesus, when He sits on the throne of glory and He will separate one from the other just a shepherd divides his sheep from the goats. The 'sheep' refers to the saved ones, who had their salvation during the period, when the Lord with His chaste bride is in the air, and likewise the 'goats' refers to the unsaved ones.

The King, who is our Lord and Savior Jesus Christ, will then say unto those, who are on His right hand, 'Come, ye blessed of my Father' and then, the King, who is our Lord and Savior Jesus Christ, will say then say unto those, who are on his left hand, 'Depart from me, ye cursed, into everlasting fire, prepared for devils and his angels'. This judgment is also known as 'sheep and goat' judgment, when the nations (gentiles) are judged.

The words of the King at this judgment are very sharp and shrewd. To those, who are on His right hand, the King will say that when He was hungry they gave Him meat, and He was hungry they gave Him drink, and when he was a stranger, they took Him; Naked, and they clothed Him, and when He was sick they visited Him, when He was in prison, they went to see Him.

The righteous on the right side of the King will be filled with the surprise and ask the King, when He was hungry,

Israel and The Church

thirsty, naked, sick and in prison. "And the King shall answer and say unto them, Verily I say unto you, Inasmuch as ye have done it unto one of the least of these my brethren, ye have done it unto me". (Matthew 25:40).

Similarly, the King, who is our Lord and Savior Jesus Christ will say very sharp and shrewd words to those, who are on His left side, that they did not give Him food when He was hungry, that they did not give him water when He was thirsty, that they did not take Him in when He was stranger, that they did not clothe him when He was naked, that they did not visit Him when He was sick, that they did not minister unto Him when He was in prison. Those, whom the Word of God, calls as 'goats', (unsaved) ones, ask Him surprisingly, when they did not gave Him drink, food, and when was He naked that they did not clothe Him, and when was He stranger that they did not take Him in, and when He was sick that they did not minister unto Him, and when was in prison, that they did not minister unto Him.

"Then shall he answer them, saying, Verily I say unto you, Inasmuch as ye did it not to one of the least of these, ye did it not to me" (Matthew 25:45)

The blessings that the King shall give unto the righteous are that they will 'inherit the kingdom prepared for you from the foundation of the world' and the punishment the King renders unto those, who are not saved will be 'Depart from me, ye cursed, into everlasting fire, prepared for the devil and his angels'.

(5). THE JUDGEMENT OF THE WICKED

And I saw a great white throne, and him that sat on it, from whose face the earth and the heaven fled away; and there was found no place for them. And I saw the dead, small and great, stand before God; and the books were opened: and another book was opened, which is the book of life: and the dead were judged out of those things which were written in the books, according to their works. (Revelation 20:11-12)

This is the 'Great White Throne judgment', which is the final judgment, where everyone, whose name is not found in the book of life is judged and 'death and hell will be cast into the lake of fire. This is the second death'. (Rev. 20:14)

Israel and The Church

CHAPTER 26 TEMPLE IN MILLENNIUM

And the man said unto me, Son of man, behold with thine eyes, and hear with thine ears, and set thine heart upon all that I shall shew thee; for to the intent that I might shew them unto thee art thou brought hither: declare all that thou seest to the house of Israel. (Ezekiel 40:4)

Bible presents to us the details of five temples. Israelites had the Tabernacle when they were journeying from Egypt to Canaan. Thereafter, the first temple was built by Solomon, the Second one was built under the supervision of Zerubbabel, son of Shealtiel, and Jeshua the son of Josedech, the third one was by Herod, the fourth one will be built by Antichrist, and fifth one by the Lord Jesus Christ, offspring of Jesse and David.

Ezekiel Chapters 40-48 give us the details of a temple, which is not the 'Tabernacle', or the First Temple (Solomon's Temple') or the Second Temple (Zerubbabel's Temple), or the Temple to be built by Antichrist. From the description and the details of construction of the temple that Ezekiel prophesied according to the word of the LORD it is clear that it is distinct from the Tabernacle and other temples.

Second Coming of Jesus

There is no word viz. "Millennium" in the Bible. However, thousand-year-reign of Lord Jesus Christ is commonly referred to as "Millennium". Revelation Chapter 20 presents the details of millennial rule of Lord Jesus Christ.

Prophet Isaiah prophesied about a period, wherein mankind will have total peace, and the length of his days on this earth is much greater than we do have now.

God says He will create new heavens and a new earth, and the present heaven and the earth will not be remembered. None of the inhabitants of the earth during that period will ever remember that there was an earth where we live now; nor will it occur to their minds that there was such an earth before they lived. The LORD will create Jerusalem to be a delight and its people a joy and He will rejoice over Jerusalem and joy over His people.

There will not be weeping or crying during those days. There will neither be 'infant-days' nor old man, who has not completed his days. Youth will not die before they complete one hundred years of age, and if there is a sinner of less than one hundred years of age, he will be considered as cursed. The inhabitants will build houses but one time; they will plant vineyards but one time, and reap the benefits of their labor entire life.

They will neither build their homes repeatedly nor will they plant again and again. The life span of the trees will be equal to the lifespan of the LORD's people. The fruit of their one time labor is enough for them to reap the benefits of such labor all their lifetime. Unlike the ground that is cursed now, because of Adam's transgression, the land in the millennial period would not be like the one that is cursed to bring forth thorns and thistles, and the labor of the inhabitants of the millennial period will not go in vain.

There will neither be extreme threat nor will there be fear; but they rejoice always because they are the seed of blessed Jehovah. Their offspring would be as much blessed as they are. The LORD will ever be present with them, and their prayers answered instantaneously. They see answers to their prayers even while they are speaking to the LORD in prayer.

The intermingling of animals and their feeding will be entirely different from that of the present animals. Wolf and lamb feed together, lion will eat straw like an ox. However, the serpent's meat will be dust as at present, because it was cursed by the LORD to be so for ever and ever, when it deceived the first man and the woman on this earth. The serpent cannot harm anyone in His holy mountain (cf. Isaiah 65:17-25).

In this period of thousand-year-reign of Lord Jesus Christ, when peace and tranquility prevails the LORD helps His people to build a magnificent temple for them to offer sacrifices and oblations to Him. The question is why would they need temple and offer sacrifices?

There shall be no more thence an infant of days, nor an old man that hath not filled his days: for the child shall die an hundred years old; but the sinner being an hundred years old shall be accursed. (Isaiah 65:20)

Notice the second part of Isaiah 65:20. It says "*but the sinner being an hundred years old shall be accursed*".

God has shown to man that in every dispensation man has come short of the glory of God, and no surprise even when full peace is afforded and extreme joy is given to man, he shows that he is unworthy of God's love. It is purely because of God's grace that we live; else we would have been consumed long ago. Thus, it is obvious that during the days of millennium there will be sin and sinners. If so, atonement of their sins is inevitable, and therefore, they

Israel and The Church

need temple and sacrifices. They continue to do so; because they missed the atonement of sin offered by the Lord Jesus Christ, and resisted His grace until the church is caught to be with Him for ever and ever.

In this dispensation of 'Grace period' we are saved because we accept Jesus as the Lord, and believe in our hearts that God raised Him from the dead. Lord Jesus Christ became propitiation for us and died on the cross on behalf of us and all those who believe in Him. Those who are saved are the members of the Church, which will be caught up when the Lord Himself descends from heaven "…with a shout, with the voice of the archangel, and with the trump of God: and the dead in Christ shall rise first: Then we which are alive and remain shall be caught up together with them in the clouds, to meet the Lord in the air: and so shall we ever be with the Lord" (1 Thessalonians 4:16-17)

Church is the bride of the Lord, and the bride will not be put to suffer by the bridegroom, the 'great tribulation' and, therefore, the Church will not enter into millennial kingdom, but will reign with Him for ever and ever over the inhabitants of millennial kingdom.

Blessed and holy is he that hath part in the first resurrection: on such the second death hath no power, but they shall be priests of God and of Christ, and shall reign with him a thousand years. (Revelation 20:6)

Israel and the Church are two distinct entities. The blessings of Israel are different from that of the Church. Irrespective of Jews and Gentiles, male or female, whoever accepts Jesus as their personal savior are all alike the members of the Church, which is the body of Christ, and He is the head of the Church.

All those who rise from graves, when the Lord comes again, and those alive, will receive glorified bodies, at the twinkling of an eye, and will see the Lord face to face and will be like Him. They will all be with Him for ever and ever to reign over those in the kingdom age. Jews and Gentiles, all alike, will have to accept Jesus as their personal savior to receive everlasting life, else if they die in the present age, before Jesus comes again, they will rise only at the end of the times, to stand before the 'great white throne' to be judged and will be cast into 'lake of fire' (cf. Revelation 20:14-15).

And shall cast them into a furnace of fire: there shall be wailing and gnashing of teeth. (Matthew 13:42)

Israel and The Church

And many of them that sleep in the dust of the earth shall awake, some to everlasting life, and some to shame and everlasting contempt. (Daniel 12:2)

The children of Israel, and others left behind after the church is caught up, will enter into 'great tribulation' period. They will, then, surely call upon Jesus as their Messiah, and seek His help for their redemption from the atrocities of Antichrist. Every knee shall bow and every tongue shall confess that Jesus is the Lord (Ref. Romans 14:11).

All those who accept Jesus as their Messiah after the Church is caught up, and all those from the nations that are judged at the 'sheep and goat judgment, and are asked to move to the right hand side of Lord Jesus Christ will enter into the millennial kingdom in their natural bodies as we do have now; *not* with glorified bodies.

For I was an hungered, and ye gave me meat: I was thirsty, and ye gave me drink: I was a stranger, and ye took me in: Naked, and ye clothed me: I was sick, and ye visited me: I was in prison, and ye came unto me. (Matthew 25:35-36)

And the King shall answer and say unto them, Verily I say unto you, Inasmuch as ye have done it unto one of the least of these my brethren, ye have done it unto me. (Matthew 25:40)

Those who were moved to the left hand side of the Lord during 'judgment of nations' also called 'Sheep and Goat judgment' will be cast into the 'lake of fire'. The reason for their fatal end would be because they refused to accept Jesus as their savior before the Church is caught up, and thereafter, never helped any Jew during the 'great tribulation' period, when beloved of the LORD were under the severe persecution from Antichrist.

For I was an hungered, and ye gave me no meat: I was thirsty, and ye gave me no drink: I was a stranger, and ye took me not in: naked, and ye clothed me not: sick, and in prison, and ye visited me not. Then shall they also answer him, saying, Lord, when saw we thee an hungered, or athirst, or a stranger, or naked, or sick, or in prison, and did not minister unto thee? Then shall he answer them, saying, Verily I say unto you, Inasmuch as ye did it not to one of the least of these, ye did it not to me. And these shall go away into everlasting punishment: but the righteous into life eternal. (Matthew 25:42-46)

Two different entities are, thus seen very clearly. One is the bride which is the Church that belongs to Lord Jesus Christ. The second one is Israel that refused to accept

Israel and The Church

Jesus as their Messiah before the bride is united with her bridegroom. In the millennial period Israel that enters into the 'kingdom of heaven' will have Lord Jesus as their king and they will be ruled by Him and the Church, which was caught up and conformed to His image.

Israel was blessed and will continue to be as a nation of blessed people with all their blessings promised to Abraham. They will worship the Lord in the same manner as they did during the period when the "Tabernacle" was among them. They will offer sacrifices and oblations to the LORD in the same manner as they did in the Old Testament period.

CHAPTRER 27 LOOKING TOWARD JERUSALEM

"Now when Daniel knew that the writing was signed, he went into his house; and his windows being open in his chamber toward Jerusalem, he kneeled upon his knees three times a day, and prayed, and gave thanks before his God, as he did aforetime" Daniel 6:10

It is very interesting to note that Daniel opened the windows of his chamber toward Jerusalem, knelt down and prayed confessing the sins of children of Israel.

"O Lord, hear; O Lord, forgive; O Lord, hearken and do; defer not, for thine own sake, O my God: for thy city and thy people are called by thy name" Daniel 9:19

The LORD heard Daniel's prayers and answered him. The children of Israel in captivity cried saying

"How shall we sing the LORD'S song in a strange land? If I forget thee, O Jerusalem, let my right hand forget [her cunning]. If I do not remember thee, let my tongue cleave to the roof of my mouth" Psalm 137:4-6

Israel and The Church

The LORD's answering to Solomon was conditional and the LORD said to Solomon that if they turned away from the LORD, His commandments and worshipped other gods He would pluck them up by the roots and will cast them out of His sight that they would become a proverb and a byword among nations (Ref. 2 Chronicles 7:19-20)

However, the promise made by God to David remains. The promise was that God will establish Solomon's kingdom forever and the LORD will be his father. If commits iniquity the LORD will chasten with rod of men and stripes of men but His mercy shall not depart away from him.

"He shall build an house for my name, and I will stablish the throne of his kingdom for ever. I will be his father, and he shall be my son. If he commit iniquity, I will chasten him with the rod of men, and with the stripes of the children of men: But my mercy shall not depart away from him, as I took it from Saul, whom I put away before thee" (2 Samuel 7:13-15)

Not long after this prayer of Solomon his kingdom declined and fell down beyond recognition because Solomon himself did that which was unpleasant to God. Israel was divided into two kingdoms – the Northern Kingdom ruled by Jeroboam and the Southern Kingdom ruled by Rehoboam, son of Solomon. Northern Kingdom consisted of the ten tribes and the Southern Kingdom consisted of Judah and Benjamin. Levites merged on both the sides.

CHAPTER 28 GRACE ABOUNDS

SIN SHALL NOT HAVE DOMINION

"And God is able to make all grace abound toward you; that ye, always having all sufficiency in all things, may abound to every good work" (2 Corinthians 9:8)

Sin shall not have dominion over born-again child because he is not under the law, but under grace. By one man's disobedience many were made sinners and so by the obedience of one shall be many made righteous. The righteousness does not confine to only many as few understand, but to all those who confess their sins to God and accept Jesus as their personal Savior. The law pointed the guilt of a person but the salvation is through the grace by faith in Jesus Christ. In him alone is salvation and there is no other way for being with him for ever and ever. Where sin abounded grace did much more abound and that is the reason why no matter how serious is the sin a man may have committed, except for blasphemy of the Holy Spirit, there is forgiveness in Jesus. Sin brought death but grace from Jesus gives us eternal life. Jesus Christ is our Lord and he is faithful to forgive us our sins.

What shall we say then, should we continue in sin that grace may abound. Apostle Paul says "God forbid". We who are dead to sin will not live in sin any longer. We are baptized into Jesus Christ into his death. (Romans 5:19-21 and Romans 6:1-3)

Those who seek to do good works and earn salvation by their own works do nullify the importance of blood of Jesus Christ. The blood of Jesus Christ that cleanses the sin has no value for them. They diligently keep doing good works in order to receive salvation neglecting the repeated emphasis from the Lord Jesus Christ that there is eternal life only in and through him. As we read in 2 Corinthians 9:8 God is able to make grace abound to every good work. But good works are not the way for salvation. The good works follow when a man is born-again.

The blood of Jesus shed on the cross of Calvary can only save a person. This is the only way to receive eternal life. Salvation is available to all those who go to him and accept him as the Lord.

Now, here is the question :

After having been delivered from the bondage of sin by grace through faith should a child of God keep sinning because he is under the grace but not under law?

Israel and The Church

No. Never should a child of God return to sin and lose blessings from God. Salvation is not lost for those who are saved in the blood of Jesus Christ; however, the Scripture does not endorse repeated sinning. God will surely chide and chastise the one that falls repeatedly into sin and seeks grace time and again.

Should we not consider the fact that if we yield to sin we are servants to sin; and sin becomes our master? We are under grace and we should remain servants to our Lord and be obedient to put on Christ as written in Ephesians 4:24.

We were, once servants of sin; but after accepting Jesus as our master, we have become servants of righteousness. We should bear fruit unto the Lord by leading a life of holiness and have assurance that there is everlasting life for us in eternity. The law has concluded all of us under sin, but the gift of God is eternal life through Lord Jesus Christ.

"And that ye put on the new man, which after God is created in righteousness and true holiness". (Ephesians 4:24)

HAS GOD CAST AWAY HIS PEOPLE

"For I would not, brethren, that ye should be ignorant of this mystery, lest ye should be wise in your own conceits\; that blindness in part is happened to Israel, until the fulness of the Gentiles be come in\" (Romans 11:25)

Apostle Paul wonders if God cast away his people and immediately reaffirms that it was not so. He says he was also of the seed of Abraham, of the tribe of Benjamin. God did not cast away his people whom he foreknew. Even when Elias was taking pride in himself that he was alone available to intercede on behalf of Israel God said to him that He had reserved seven thousand men unto him who could intercede on behalf of Israel.

If the salvation, therefore, is by "grace", then it is not by "works". What then happened exactly that their attitude and belief has not changed yet? Yes, it is because God blinded their eyes for a season and gave them spiritual slumber that they should not see and that they may not have ears for hearing unto this day. Have Israel stumbled that they should fall then? Apostle Paul himself answers these questions (Romans 11th Chapter) that God did not blind them or made them deaf because they were

Israel and The Church

stumbling blocks nor was it because they have stumbled, but because of God's desire that everyone in the world, irrespective of Jews or Gentiles be saved and have eternal life.

Apostle Paul explains elaborately the plan of God for the salvation of Gentiles in Romans 11th Chapter. Jews always insisted on recompensing God's favor with their own good works in order to earn salvation. They thought that their Messiah would come like a king. It is because of their misunderstanding that salvation is come unto the Gentiles.

"That at that time ye were without Christ, being aliens from the commonwealth of Israel, and strangers from the covenants of promise, having no hope, and without God in the world: But now in Christ Jesus ye who sometimes were far off are made nigh by the blood of Christ" (Ephesians 2:12-13)

CHAPTER 29 THE FATHER'S LOVE

"Behold, what manner of love the Father hath bestowed upon us, that we should be called the sons of God: therefore the world knoweth us not, because it knew him not. Beloved, now are we the sons of God, and it doth not yet appear what we shall be: but we know that, when he shall appear, we shall be like him; for we shall see him as he is". (1 John 3:1-2)

Every human parent loves his children and children love their parents; however, the love the Father has bestowed lavishly on the children of God is incomparable. We, as human beings have limitations. The love of the Father is too great to measure its height and its depth cannot be fathomed. He has separated us from our sins as Far East is from the West.

It is usual that we do not give importance to that which we see or hear quite often. It flows into our lives as if it was normal or we are entitled to such benefits and privileges. A motorbike making unusual sound every day while on a nearby road may not become as one that makes annoying noise. Our ears grow immune to such regular recurring noises. Similarly, a man hearing very often about God's love may become immune to the proclamation of it and would feel it is normal and he thinks that he deserves to have such love.

Behold what manner of love the Father has so lavishly bestowed on us. Ponder on the manner of love and the greatness of that love that the Father has bestowed on us. Only when we make a serious study of Father's love we realize how great it is.

"Thus saith the LORD, In an acceptable time have I heard thee, and in a day of salvation have I helped thee: and I will preserve thee, and give thee for a covenant of the people, to establish the earth, to cause to inherit the desolate heritages" (Isaiah 49:8)

In spite of Father forgiving the children Israel their complaint was "The LORD hath forsaken me, and my Lord hath forgotten me". But the LORD says to them "Can a woman forget her sucking child, that she should not have compassion on the son of her womb? yea, they may forget, yet will I not forget thee. Behold, I have graven thee upon the palms of my hands; thy walls are continually before me" (cf. Isaiah 49:13-17)

God so loved the world that He gave His only begotten Son for our sake. It pleased the Father to bruise Him on the cross for our sake in order that we may be saved. However, many do not realize the greatness of the sacrifice of Lord Jesus Christ on the cross to save us from destruction. Has God given the privilege to everyone to become His children? No, John Chapter 1 vs. 12 has the answer.

"But as many as received him, to them gave he power to become the sons of God, even to them that believe on his name" (John 1:12)

To all those who believe in Lord Jesus Christ, the Son of God, the Father has given the privilege to call Him as "Abba, Father". It is no small privilege for Christians to call the God of heaven as "Father". The greatest privilege a Christian can have is to be adopted into His family. Even Adam did not have that kind of privilege. The relationship between God and those who are born again is so great that He calls them that believe in Him as the 'sons of God'.

"For as many as are led by the Spirit of God, they are the sons of God. For ye have not received the spirit of bondage again to fear; but ye have received the Spirit of adoption, whereby we cry, Abba, Father. The Spirit itself beareth witness with our spirit, that we are the children of

Israel and The Church

God: And if children, then heirs; heirs of God, and joint-heirs with Christ; if so be that we suffer with him, that we may be also glorified together" (Romans 8:14-17)

Imagine If God took a sympathetic attitude on our depraved condition rather than love us we would not have had the privilege of becoming 'sons of God'. We now realize that God's love has greater relevance to our salvation.

Compare the love of the earthly father of the prodigal son in the parable Jesus narrated. The father of the prodigal son could have very well taken a sympathetic attitude, rather than love him when he returned home, repenting that he spent his entire portion of wealth on trivial things of life and then when he had nothing to spend he was ready to eat food that was meant for pigs.

Father of the prodigal son could have sympathized and given him place to stay in his outhouse as a servant, or have any other position sans the wealth he already procured as his inheritance from the father. He could, perhaps provide him some clothing, and some food as well. But it was not so, the father loved prodigal son, embraced him and put on him the best robe, put a ring on his hand, shoes on his feet, and ordered his servants to bring a fatted calf and kill it, eat and be merry. The father said his son was dead and was alive again; he was lost and was found. May we truly understand as to how much more our heavenly Father loves us? (cf. Luke 15:11-32).

It was this kind of love that God showed towards us when we were drowned in miry clay of sin like swine enjoying to be in the dirty pond. God sent His only begotten Son for our sake. Lord Jesus Christ took the form of a servant in the likeness of man relinquishing His glory with the Father, in order to bear

our sin upon Him and die for us, even the death on the cross, which was most humiliating death.

The Father in heaven is calling those sinners who have not yet repented of their sins to confess their sins to Lord Jesus Christ and accept Him as their personal Savior. Those who have already accepted Lord Jesus Christ as their personal Savior may realize the love of the Father and not commit sins because the word of God says whoever commits sin is of the devil; and there is no such temptation which is beyond man's control to overcome it; rather with every temptation which Satan brings in a believer's life, there comes also an escape route which

Israel and The Church

God provides to overcome it. (cf. 1 John 3:8, 1 Corinthians 10:18)

The Father in heaven promised believers in Christ that they will be conformed to the image of His Son and we shall be like Him when He shall appear and we shall see Him as He is (cf. Romans 8:29, 1 John 3:2)

"For whom he did foreknow, he also did predestinate to be conformed to the Image of his Son, that he might be the firstborn among many brethren" (Romans 8:29)

"Beloved, now are we the sons of God, and it doth not yet appear what we shall be: but we know that, when he shall appear, we shall be like him; for we shall see him as he is". (1 John 3:2)

CHAPTER 30 NEW NAME FOR JERUSALEM

The Holy city Jerusalem, the city of our Lord, is now filled with political turmoil with no peace among the dwellers in the city. The city walls are broken down and no one can surely identify where "Zion" is. Zerubbabel Temple, which was renovated and named as "Herod's Temple" was destroyed and not a stone was left one upon another as prophesied by Lord Jesus Christ.

"And Jesus said unto them, See ye not all these things? verily I say unto you, There shall not be left here one stone upon another, that shall not be thrown down" (Matthew 24:2)

There is "dome of the rock" under Islamic control, and rebuilding the Temple has become a serious controversial issue. But, the day will come when the city will be called "Hephzibah", and its land "Beulah". The Lord delights in making the city delightful for every one and the land like married woman. (Isaiah Ch. 62:4). This is a prophecy about the status of Jerusalem in the millennial kingdom of Jesus.

Israel and The Church

Lord Jesus Christ is the Messiah. The Jews rejected him and called upon themselves the blood of Jesus in order that he may be crucified (Matthew 27:24-25). Peter's speech testifies about those who crucified Jesus.

"Ye men of Israel, hear these words; Jesus of Nazareth, a man approved of God among you by miracles and wonders and signs, which God did by him in the midst of you, as ye yourselves also know: Him, being delivered by the determinate counsel and foreknowledge of God, ye have taken, and by wicked hands have crucified and slain" (Acts 2:22-23)

Indeed, they paid the price in AD 70 according to historians. Earlier, they worshipped idols many-a-time and were chastised by God. They rebelled against God and paid the price for their actions. Yet, they are his people; the city of David is his city.

Like Boaz, who was kinsman redeemer of Ruth, Jesus is our redeemer. He came into this world, died for our sins, was buried, rose from the dead on the third day and later ascended into heaven. He is seated on the right hand of the Majesty and interceding for us. We, who are redeemed by the blood of Christ, are greater than the unrepentant Jews. But for those, who have accepted Jesus as their

Second Coming of Jesus

personal savior, there is no condemnation irrespective of their race, ethnicity, color, or creed.

Lord Jesus, who is the messiah, speaks and says that he will not sit quite, nor will he rest until he redeems city of Jerusalem again. He defeats the kings loyal to Antichrist at "Armageddon", and sits on the throne of David and literally rules. In the thousand years of his rule there shall be perfect peace. Satan will be bound with chains and thrown into abyss by an angel who comes from heaven. Later Satan will be released for a short time when he goes Gog and Magog to deceive the nations but fire from God comes down from heaven and devours Satan. (Revelation Ch. 20:8)

The dead who did not accept Jesus Christ as their personal savior will resurrect at that time. The Lord shall judge them at the 'Great white throne' and cast them along with death, hell, and the devil and his angels into the 'lake of fire' to be tormented for ever and ever. This is the second death. For those who are saved, there is no second death but they will have everlasting life to be with the Lord for ever and ever.

Israel and The Church

Note here when Antichrist and false prophet are thrown into the lake of fire! It is before the devil that deceived!!! Revelation 20:10 confirms it. When the devil was cast into the lake of fire, the Antichrist and the false prophet were already there in the lake of fire. These are only the ones who will be in the lake of fire before the 'Great White Throne Judgment' (Revelation 16:16 and Revelation 20:8-10). Does the Scripture say anybody is thrown into the lake of fire before Antichrist and false prophet. No, not at all!

There shall come out of heaven a New Jerusalem and we, who are saved, shall be in that Holy City. The Church is the bride of our Lord Jesus Christ. Lord Jesus says that he has set watchmen upon the walls of Jerusalem and they will not keep quite nor will sleep but keep a watch over the city and will make the city a praise of the earth. This is a promise of Messiah and he has sworn by his right hand and by the arm of his strength. Messiah promised that no more the enemies of Jerusalem will eat its corn as their food no stranger will ever drink its wine. Gentiles will see its righteousness and kings will glory.

"And the Gentiles shall see thy righteousness, and all kings thy glory: and thou shalt be called by a new name, which the mouth of the LORD shall name." (Isaiah 62:2)

Second Coming of Jesus

Israel and The Church

www.ingramcontent.com/pod-product-compliance
Lightning Source LLC
Chambersburg PA
CBHW071456040426
42444CB00008B/1356